CRICKLEY MEADOW

***

***

GERARD CLARK

ILLUSTRATIONS

BY

EILEEN BRISCOE

*We at Trafford believe that it is the responsibility of us all, as both individuals
and corporations, to make choices that are environmentally and socially sound.
You, in turn, are supporting this responsible conduct each time you purchase a
Trafford book, or make use of our publishing services. To find out how you are
helping, please visit www.trafford.com/responsiblepublishing.html*

*Our mission is to efficiently provide the world's finest, most comprehensive
book publishing service, enabling every author to experience success.
To find out how to publish your book, your way, and have it available
worldwide, visit us online at www.trafford.com*

Trafford rev. 10/19/2009

 www.trafford.com

North America & international
toll-free: 1 888 232 4444 (USA & Canada)
phone: 250 383 6864 ♦ fax: 812 355 4082 ♦ email: info@trafford.com

For Christine, Andy and Joe.

A very special thank you to Mick and Maggie Cronin, Bethany McCrave and Eileen Briscoe for their critique, ideas and suggestions and also to the little furry creatures that provided the inspiration for the characters in this story.

CHAPTER ONE

FERNBROOK COTTAGE

The first glimmer of light shone through the outhouse window one late August morning and, as the birds began to sing, another *early bird* was slowly stirring with one thought on his mind—breakfast! The black shorthaired cavy with white bands of fur around his neck and midriff and a distinctive white *V* running the length of his distinctively long nose, ambled towards the food bowl.

'Snff, mm, not much in here,' he muttered to himself, 'I wonder if...?'

'Oh Sniffer!' called Jessie, who by now had also stirred from her slumber, 'if you're looking for carrots you're going to be out of luck—you polished them off last night—*remember?*'

'Oh yes, I suppose I did,' muttered Sniffer disappointedly.

Jessie was a black *self*, or in other words one-coloured, shorthaired cavy. She was only too aware of Sniffer's love of carrots and was thankful that she wasn't all that keen on them herself as there were *never* any left over.

'Snff, I suppose I'll just have to make do with a bit of muesli,' grumbled poor old Sniffer.

'Well you're not going to fade away,' laughed Jessie who had become used to Sniffer's ways, having shared a hutch with him since her arrival from the local pet shop.

She used to think that he was fonder of carrots than he was of her—he certainly seemed to show more interest in them! For a long time Jessie had wondered if she was ever going to have a litter. The cause of Sniffer's unusual behaviour one hot summer's day about fourteen months ago, will forever remain a mystery but Jessie went on to have her first litter early that autumn.

Jessie and Sniffer became the proud parents of Boo, Badger and Gnasher. They were bouncing healthy babies although Gnasher *did* have to go to the vets for a minor operation. It came as less of a surprise when Jessie had her second litter of Joey and Emily not too long afterwards. Believing then that her childbearing days had been put firmly behind her, Jessie should have known to expect the unexpected where Sniffer was concerned. She was now expecting her third litter at any time!

Sniffer was not the most energetic of creatures and his happiest moments were spent munching on a carrot as he watched the world go by. He certainly did not seek excitement or adventure in his life. Jessie sometimes showed a little annoyance at his apparent laziness and general inertia but in truth, she wouldn't have wanted him any other way.

Sniffer's offspring had certainly not inherited his laid-back traits— indeed Badger and Gnasher displayed an abundance of energy. However, if anyone harboured doubts that the pair shared Sniffer's genes, their qualms were soon dispelled with one glance at Gnasher's long nose—the resemblance to Sniffer's was unmistakeable!

The outhouse was situated in the back garden of Fernbrook Cottage in the village of Crickley Meadow, about three miles from the town of Whitebridge. Fernbrook Cottage was home to Mr and Mrs Fitchett *and* to thirty cavies, or as these creatures are more popularly known, guinea pigs.

The longest-standing outhouse residents were Cedric and Misty, both having arrived just over three years ago. Sniffer and Smokey came along soon afterwards on the same day as each other. Smokey, who had a hutch to herself, was semi-longhaired and mostly smoky-brown in colour with a small distinguishing light brown line across her nose. A light marking around her eyes contrasted with a darker shade, giving her the appearance of a koala bear. Having heard the *goings on* next door Smokey realised that she might be in a position to help out.

'Sniffer,' she cried, 'I've got a carrot left over from last night— would you like it?'

Sniffer immediately looked across to where the voice was coming from and responded excitedly.

'Oh, yes please Smokey!'

Smokey just happened to have a big juicy carrot left on her plate. She would have eaten it in her own time but she was more partial to cabbage and lettuce and could see that Sniffer's need was greater than hers. She had noticed Sniffer's *plight* while preening herself to ensure that her coat was in tip-top condition and that no hairs were out of place in her tuft.

'How are you going to get it over here?' Sniffer asked with a sudden tinge of apprehension.

Smokey didn't live in a conventional hutch. Hers was an open-top pen that contained a small *house* as her living quarters.

'Just watch!' she replied.

She took the carrot in her teeth, drew back her head and, with a commendable effort, flicked it over the top of her pen in the direction of Sniffer and Jessie's hutch.

Sniffer watched with baited breath as the airborne vegetable looped towards the wire mesh of his front door.

'Come on, come on!' he muttered to himself, just before the tapered end of the flying orange root landed lengthways and lodged itself perfectly in one of the squares of the mesh. Sniffer thanked Smokey gleefully as he dragged the carrot inside.

'Nice shot ma!' drawled a voice from nearby.

The voice in question was that of Smokey's son Charlie who lived next door to her with his hutch-mate Patrick. Charlie and Patrick were born at Fernbrook Cottage around the same time as each other, Patrick being the offspring of Misty. The pair had shared a hutch since they were just a few weeks old. Charlie, who was shorthaired and self buff-coloured with albino eyes, curiously always wore a trilby hat and spoke in a mid-American drawl. Patrick, an American crested brown and buff shorthaired guinea pig, always likened Charlie's behaviour to that of a gangster. Charlie often tried to terrorise the younger guinea pigs out in the garden by finding a stick and pretending it was a tommy gun, but they have all become used to him now and either humour him or just tell him to go away.

Patrick, in his soft Irish brogue, had once asked Smokey if she knew what made Charlie behave the way he did—and why he spoke with that accent.

'I'm not absolutely certain,' Smokey had told Patrick, before she went on to say, 'mind you, I've often thought that it might have something to do with that film about Al Capone that Mr and Mrs Fitchett were watching when we were in the maternity hutch—and then there was that James Cagney movie as well.'

The *maternity hutch* was a special hutch that was taken indoors and kept in the Fitchett's living room whenever a *sow* was expecting, so that they could be given extra special care. Patrick couldn't even remember being *in* the maternity hutch, never mind noticing what was on the telly.

'Say Paddy,' called Charlie, gesturing with his head towards the large hutch situated next door and at a right angle to their own, 'check that out!'

The reference was to Pauline who lived there with her three daughters. Pauline was black and white and shorthaired with ample childbearing hips and had been known to turn many a head in her time. She had already been expecting a litter when a local family gave her to the Fitchetts.

Pauline had decided to get up early this particular morning so that she could get to use the mirror first instead of waiting an age for her three daughters, Monica, Maisie and Tufty, to be finished with it. She looked at her pretty face and at the smooth white fur that ran the length of her nose, though differed from Sniffers in that it branched outwards over her eyes to give the appearance of eyebrows. The rest of her was black apart from a white band behind her neck. Although Pauline would never have said it out loud, she couldn't help thinking that she wasn't half bad looking for her age.

'Oh, mum's hogging the mirror,' moaned Tufty.

'Still, we could always use Monica as a mirror,' laughed Maisie a little unkindly. She was referring to Monica's smooth, black shiny coat that shimmered when she moved.

'Good idea,' agreed Tufty.

'Ha, ha, very funny,' snapped Monica, 'don't forget, it's *me* the Fitchetts have decided to show in the autumn fair!'

'You never *let* us forget it!' Maisie fired back.

They all had their mother's good looks and the four of them undoubtedly provided the glamour at Fernbrook Cottage.

Charlie and Patrick, their hutch being so close to the girls, were always looking to attract their attention and make an impression but this invariably met with little success. It didn't help their cause that nearly all the other grown-up males fancied their chances as well and this had an unfortunate tendency to swell the girls' heads a little.

Not least of their admirers was Cedric who, as usual, was one of the last to rise on this particular morning. Cedric was English crested, longhaired and predominantly dark brown in colour. Being English crested, his tuft was white, in contrast to his American crested cousins whose tufts blend in with the rest of their fur. He had been rescued by the Fitchetts from a life of animal experimentation and now shared a hutch with his son Cyril.

Cedric lost no time in going to his specially designed fireproof compartment to light up his first cigarette of the day. As he drew the putrefying smoke down into his lungs he reflected on the last few glorious weeks when the weather had been hot and sunny most of the time, and on how this had given all the animals the chance to play out in the garden just about every day. Today was going to be fine once again and they would almost certainly be let out to enjoy the wonderful garden at Fernbrook Cottage.

The long-suffering, passive smoking Cyril was very like Cedric in appearance except that his coat was ginger, but he was much the more sensibly behaved of the two.

'Dad?' he called out.

'What son?'

'I hate to sound as if I'm nagging but why do you have to smoke those…things?'

'I'm sorry son,' replied Cedric in a genuinely remorseful tone, 'I really wish I could give them up but the thing is *I need them!*'

'Yes I'm sure you do,' Cyril went on, his eyes watering a little, 'but what about the damage it's doing to your lungs?'

'Why does everyone have to make such a fuss?—it's not as if they're doing me any real harm,' wheezed Cedric, before breaking into a fit of coughing.

'Couldn't you at least try to give up?' pleaded Cyril, with very little optimism.

'I'd really like to, but you'll never understand just how hard it is. I wish they'd never put me in that laboratory, making me smoke all those cigarettes every day. I absolutely hated it and I was barely a youth, it was so unfair. When the Fitchetts rescued me I planned to stop but I found I was missing them too much and I was getting terrible withdrawals. It's lucky for me that I was allowed to carry on smoking even if they *are* rationed.'

'Oh well, maybe one day eh dad?'

'Hope so son, but don't hold your breath,' came the spluttered reply.

Now Cedric was a bit of a lady's pig and he particularly fancied his chances with Pauline and her daughters, although his wolf-whistles and constant remarks to the girls out in the garden never cut any ice. He would often try and flatter Pauline by asking her how her sisters were when he was, of course, referring to her daughters.

Although he never seemed to notice it, Cedric's antics did affect one female. Misty, who was American crested with smooth, rusty coloured hair, had not shared a hutch with anyone since losing her first partner Harold, although her daughters, Mandy and Gracie lived in the hutch next door while her son Patrick, of course, lived close by.

In the long hours spent in the garden, Misty had gradually found herself growing closer to Cedric during the course of their many chats together although she had no idea whether her feelings were reciprocated. She was acutely aware that he was a bit of a flirt and thought that his smoking habit was disgusting. Despite what she might have expected her better judgement to be, Misty seemed to find herself looking forward to going out in the garden, mostly for those brief moments that she could snatch with Cedric. He would always stop and spend time with her but was easily distracted and would usually be off somewhere else, much to her disappointment, even though she tried to never let it show.

Cyril, however, had noticed the amount of attention that Misty was paying to his dad and had tried his hand at matchmaking.

'Misty?' Cedric had replied, 'yeah, she's a great girl but I don't think she's that keen on me and, anyway, there's too much fun to be had!'

Cedric had sired a number of offspring in his time although he was unable to keep count of precisely how many. Three of them, Cyril, Sandy and Buttons, lived at Fernbrook Cottage while the rest either lived elsewhere in Crickley Meadow or Whitebridge or even in such far-flung places as Lambourne or Over Stanley. Sandy and Buttons, like their mother Lucky, were longhaired English crested guinea pigs, Lucky and Buttons being dark brown. The buff-coloured Sandy shared a hutch with Lucky while Buttons lived next door with her *black and tan* Abyssinian friend Rosie.

Below Smokey's pen, young Freddy was calling out excitedly to his sister Dorie.

'Come on, we'll be going out on the garden soon—I'm really looking forward to playing today!'

'How can you be so sure we'll be going out?' frowned Dorie.

'We're bound to, we've been out every day for ages now!' asserted Freddy, who looked handsome with his long black hair, parted crest and white eyebrows.

These two youngsters, from Joey's first and only litter so far, lived with their mother.

'Mum?' cried Freddy, 'we *will* be going out today won't we?'

'Honestly Freddy!' replied Joey, 'you ask me that question every day and what do I always say to you?—*it's not up to me, it's up to Mrs Fitchett!*'

Freddy cried out again, this time turning in the direction of the hutch next door.

'Hey Cleo; Flossy;—are you playing hide and seek later on?'

Cleo and Flossy were also very young and lived with their mother Boo and their Auntie Emily. All four, like Joey and Dorie, were smooth-haired and white with a variety of *assorted* eye patches between them. Boo and Joey had once gone to stay for a week at another address in Crickley Meadow where two of Cedric's sons lived. Both had returned home expecting litters. Boo had two other white albino daughters from that litter but they now lived at their father's address.

Cleo and Flossy didn't answer Freddy's question but they were certainly looking forward to playing in the garden.

One incumbent was very hopeful of being allowed to go out. Miffy, a smooth, white self-coloured albino with a very pretty face had only recently been given to the Fitchetts when her previous owner moved abroad. She particularly enjoyed the opportunity it afforded her to chat with Bobby and Dylan. These dark brown Sheltie guinea pigs had also been given to the Fitchetts and shared a hutch close to Miffy's. The brothers both had light brown flecks and distinguishing long flowing hair coming down from a parting at the top of their heads, and were sometimes difficult to tell apart. Miffy never had any such trouble. She was struck by their handsome appearance but in particular, by Bobby's cool demeanour.

CHAPTER TWO

THE GARDEN

At about 9.00am the outhouse door opened and Mrs Fitchett entered, talking to her pets as she always did. They returned her greeting with a chorus of excited squeaking. This stemmed in no small part from their eager anticipation of being allowed out onto the garden.

After checking them all Mrs Fitchett announced, 'well it's another lovely day so you'll all be going out again!' They responded with more squeaking as she continued, 'and I've a surprise for you—we've got visitors arriving later!'

Mrs Fitchett was in a bit of a teasing mood this morning and, as the guinea pigs stared as if waiting for her to elaborate she added, 'you'll find out soon enough who they are.'

She then got each one of them out and placed them on the neatly trimmed lawn.

'I hope you two are going to get along today,' she said, casting Badger and Gnasher a stern glance.

The look on their faces suggested that butter wouldn't melt in their mouths but Mrs Fitchett wasn't convinced. These two brothers from Sniffer and Jessie's first litter used to share a hutch but had to be separated as they got older because of their constant fighting. Mrs Fitchett was often tending to their wounds. They now each have their own hutch but even this doesn't stop them from snarling and baring their teeth at each other.

Mrs Fitchett picked up Badger, who was smooth and white with black on both eyes and to the rear. With her other hand she collected Gnasher, who was also smooth white with black and brown patches, mostly to the right of his face and to his rear. On his lengthy nose was a black diamond with brown flecks at the tip.

'I'll be putting you two on your own in separate pens if there's any trouble!' she warned.

Before long, all thirty guinea pigs were outside enjoying the morning sunshine. Pauline, Monica, Maisie and Tufty immediately began to graze on the beautiful lawn that people often complimented Mr Fitchett on. He usually forgot to mention that he never actually put a lawnmower anywhere near the grass thanks to the work done by thirty sets of cavy teeth. He had, in fact, stopped using his electric lawnmower after Boo, Badger and Gnasher had gnawed through the cable when they were very young. That was when Mr Fitchett discovered that the tool had become redundant.

Closely behind Pauline and her daughters came Cedric, who chewed the occasional blade of grass in between keeping a close eye on the girls. With him were Cyril, Bobby, Dylan, Charlie and Patrick. Smokey, Misty, Sandy, Mandy, Lucky, Gracie, Buttons and Rosie were chatting under the shade of a conifer tree while Boo, Miffy, Joey and Emily were huddled beneath a bush. Expectant mother Jessie, who had to take things easy, went to sit in the outdoor hutch while Sniffer, who always *liked* to take things easy, joined her there.

Badger and Gnasher, by far the most energetic of them all, were variously running around, chewing grass or briefly mingling with the other groups, their influence on whom was just a little disruptive at times. Jessie would often implore Sniffer to go and sort his sons out but he perpetually dismissed their behaviour as *youthful exuberance*. You would never find Sniffer expending any more effort than was absolutely necessary.

All the while the younger ones—Dorie, Cleo, Flossy and Freddy—were springing playfully around the garden, usually engrossed in games of chase or hide and seek but sometimes joining the adults to see what they were talking about.

'Look at Bobby,' purred Miffy to her companions under the bush as she looked out across the lawn, 'isn't he just gorgeous?'

'He's ok but I like my men to be manly,' replied Emily.

'But Bobby *is* manly!' protested Miffy. 'Just because he's so cool it doesn't mean he can't be macho as well!'

'I like his brother Dylan,' sighed Joey.

'I've noticed you like the hairy type!' laughed Emily, mischievously referring to the fact that Joey had recently had a litter to one of Cedric's longhaired sons.

'How about Cedric?' Boo suggested.

'Oh Cedric's a great laugh,' replied Joey, 'but I wouldn't want to be cooped up in a hutch with him, especially with all that smoke!'

The others muttered in general agreement.

'Anyway Boo, who would be *your* type?' asked Miffy.

'Cyril's really cute—in fact he's as good looking as his dad only more sensible.'

'*Sensible*, that's the problem,' groaned Emily. 'He spends so much time worrying about Cedric that he never even *notices* any of us!'

At this point Rosie came over and joined them.

'What are you girls talking about?' she enquired nosily.

'Oh, just about the boys,' Boo answered. 'Who would be your type of boy Rosie?'

'I don't have a type and, to be honest, I'm not really interested in boys,' Rosie replied dismissively.

'Just wait till you meet your Mr Right!' Emily assured her.

'Huh, no chance!' was Rosie's response to that notion.

The young cavies were running past, chasing each other when Freddy suddenly stopped and asked; 'hey Rosie, why do you brush your coat into those tufts?'

He was referring to the rosettes that were common to all Abyssinian cavies. All the girls sniggered as Rosie informed him that she didn't brush her coat into tufts, they were like that naturally.

'Cool,' Freddy replied.

'*Freddy*,' cried out Dorie, Cleo and Flossy—'*come and find us!*'

It did not take him long to find them hiding around the other side of the conifer tree in whose shade Smokey and the other girls were sitting.

'That was too easy,' boasted Freddy, 'you always hide behind *Cuddles!*'

'What do you mean *Cuddles?*' Dorie asked.

'This tree, it's called *Cuddles*,' answered Freddy.

'How do you know that?' frowned Cleo.

'Well, look at this,' said Freddy, pointing to a label tied to the trunk of the tree with some writing on it—'it says *Cuddles!*'

'Why would anyone call a tree Cuddles?' Flossy wondered.

They were all puzzling over this when Dorie decided to ask the older girls who were sitting close by. The question was greeted with stony silence for a short while until…!

'Old grandma Cuddles!' piped up Smokey with sudden recollection. 'I haven't seen her since…well, since they put her in a hole in the ground.'

'*A hole in the ground?*' gasped the others.

'Yes, the Fitchetts put her there—it was right next to this tree if I remember rightly.'

'Who in their right mind would want to be put in a hole in the ground?' shrugged Sandy, somewhat perplexed.

'I know *I* wouldn't,' Buttons assured her.

'Nor would I,' Lucky concurred, 'it doesn't sound very nice, does it?'

The others all agreed that it sounded pretty horrible but Smokey added, 'I must say that I'm inclined to agree with you but I do remember Mrs Fitchett saying at the time that Cuddles had gone to a better place.'

'*A better place?*' gasped Gracie incredulously, 'well call me choosy but give me my hutch and lovely hay any day of the week!'

Once that had been sorted out the children were impatient to start playing again.

'Last one to *Sniffer's Rock* is a rat!' shouted Dorie to the others, before stopping in her tracks. 'Hang on! Why is it called *Sniffer's* Rock anyway?'

'Yes its odd,' agreed Cleo, 'I mean they haven't put Sniffer in a hole in the ground have they?'

Sandy explained, 'it's called *Sniffer's Rock* because Mr Fitchett put it there to cover a hole at the bottom of the fence that Sniffer had escaped through one day.'

'Yes, he was gone for hours,' added Gracie, 'the Fitchetts were searching high and low until they eventually found him sitting in the field just the other side of the fence.'

'Let's try and move the rock then we can see for ourselves what it's like outside!' Freddy shouted with great enthusiasm.

'You'll not be moving that rock anywhere!' laughed Misty, 'just you go and see how heavy it is!'

Freddy ran over to the rock shouting to Dorie, Cleo and Flossy as he went.

'Come on—let's have a go at shifting it!'

The four of them pushed themselves up against the rock and, at the count of three, heaved together with all the strength they could muster. Try as they might, the rock would not budge and, after a couple of attempts, they sat back defeated and not a little exhausted.

'I don't think that rock would move even if we had Badger, Gnasher *and* all the other grown-ups helping us!' gasped Flossy.

'What did I tell you?' shrugged Misty.

'You should listen to those older and wiser than you,' cut in Rosie, who had come back over to be amongst the action. 'Anyway, even if you *could* get outside, my advice to you would be to stay right here in the garden where it's safe!'

'So it isn't safe outside then?' asked Cleo.

'No it isn't!' snapped Rosie. 'For a start you could get lost and then there would be no one to feed you.'

'*And* you wouldn't have a hutch to live in,' added Gracie.

'Then there's all sorts of nasty creatures and horrible things out there,' Sandy chipped in.

'Yes, there are foxes,' said Mandy, 'and rats,' added Miffy.

'And dogs and cats,' contributed Lucky.

'*And there's Kurt Sting!*' hissed Rosie menacingly.

'What's Kurt Sting?' asked Dorie.

'You mean *who's* Kurt Sting?' Rosie corrected her. 'You wouldn't want to meet *him!*—he's a very bad boy. They say he likes to capture small animals and torture them and do horrible things.'

The children were cowering as they listened intently to Rosie's words.

'What kind of horrible things?' Cleo asked tentatively, even though she wasn't too sure that she wanted to hear the reply.

'It's rumoured in Whitebridge that he's kidnapped small animals and tied them up and thrown things at them,' answered Rosie.

'Thrown what exactly?' asked Cleo uneasily.

'Rocks and stones as I understand it,' Rosie replied.

'What kind of animals does he capture?' Flossy enquired apprehensively.

'Cats, I think, and maybe rabbits and...,' Rosie stopped in her tracks.

Freddy attempted to second-guess what Rosie had refrained from saying when he coyly ventured, 'guinea pigs?'

'Yes, maybe, I don't know,' answered Rosie hesitantly, not wanting to scare the children *too* much. 'Anyway, just stay in the garden and you'll be safe and sound!'

'Well Whitebridge isn't all that close is it?' asked Dorie rhetorically.

The children, needing no more convincing that they were safer staying on their side of the fence, were now quite keen to ensure that Sniffer's Rock remained exactly where it was.

'I wonder *why* Sniffer wanted to go outside?' asked Freddy to anyone who was listening.

'Yes Sniffer, why did you go outside?' Gracie called out.

'Snff, just curious,' replied Sniffer.

'But you were gone for hours, what on earth were you doing?' asked Rosie.

'Oh, just sitting and looking.'

'Looking at what?' demanded Rosie, her cynical tone leaving Sniffer in no doubt that she expected the answer to be a good one.

'Well, I was just looking at the field and snff...,' he continued with some embarrassment, 'I was imagining that it was full of carrots.'

'I might have known!' Rosie exclaimed.

'Oh Sniffer, you've got a one-track mind!' Jessie gently chided him.

'What's a *one-track mind* Dorie?' Freddy asked.

'I think it might be something that grown-ups have,' Dorie answered uncertainly.

'Oh!' said Freddy, who at that moment spotted Cedric nearby.

Cedric was still engaging in a bit of banter with Pauline's troupe although he was getting some competition from Charlie and Patrick.

Cedric dismissed their approaches. 'You two have got *no* chance— you may as well give up!'

'Is that so?—well we'll be seeing about that to be sure!' Patrick responded defiantly.

'Hey, Tufty!' Cedric called out, 'how about you and me honey?— wouldn't you like me to show you a good time?'

'In your dreams!' Tufty replied, giggling with the other girls.

'Oh come on baby, you've got the body of an angel—give us a break!'

Just then Freddy came over to Cedric and called out, *'Grandad?'*

'What is it youngster?' Cedric asked as he continued to make a play for Tufty.

'Do you know something?—*you've got a one-track mind!*'

Freddy failed to appreciate the admonishing tone of his delivery.

'Eh…what?' Cedric muttered, scratching his head in bemusement.

Just then Mrs Fitchett came out to place *dinner* in the middle of the lawn. The lettuce, cabbage, celery and carrots, along with the dandelion leaves that she had picked from a nearby field, soon attracted the attention of all the animals who began squeaking as they came over to choose from what was on offer.

Sniffer, predictably, went straight for the carrots, as did some of the other males, while Smokey decided to start with a cabbage leaf. The dandelion leaves had grown to a good length and Joey, Emily, Miffy, Patrick, Bobby and Dylan were tucking into a pile of them. Badger was eating whatever Gnasher was eating and Gnasher vice versa. When Badger started on a lettuce leaf, Gnasher would try to pull it off him and then when Gnasher found a cabbage leaf, Badger decided it would be a good idea to claim it for himself.

'Can't you two even *eat* without arguing?' sighed Rosie. 'Obviously not,' she muttered when Badger and Gnasher did not answer her but just carried on as they had been doing.

The dandelion leaves were just about all gone and only Miffy and Bobby were still chewing them. They were nibbling away so intently that neither noticed that they were both chewing the same leaf until they reached the middle and their mouths met.

'Ooh!' exclaimed Miffy with a little embarrassment but even more excitement.

'Oh, sorry,' apologised Bobby, 'I didn't notice you were so close.'

'That's alright,' cooed Miffy as Bobby added, 'we'll have to stop meeting like this.'

Miffy was still thinking about her *brief encounter* when Mrs Fitchett came back out to inform them that their visitors were just arriving.

— CHAPTER THREE —

A FIENDISH PLOT

Cuthbert Fanshaw was sitting in his office at Fanshaw Cosmetics, pondering a rather difficult problem. His company specialised in the development of cosmetics and toiletries and had a laboratory at the site just outside Whitebridge, together with a factory and warehouse. The operation had suffered a setback in recent months after being forced to stop the animal testing that it had always relied upon. At first Cuthbert had chosen to ignore the huge public outcry against the testing but, as the protesters became more organised, they began to make life very difficult for him.

On one particular day about six months ago, many protesters and some of their pets arrived at the gates of Fanshaw Cosmetics. Mr and Mrs Fitchett had helped to organise the protest and had brought Bobby and Boo along with them. Some people were holding up placards while others had photographs of animals that were being used for testing.

One showed a picture of a rabbit with eyes that were red and sore after having drops put in them. Mrs Fitchett held up a photo of a guinea pig that had had its back shaved so that cosmetics could be tested on its skin. A placard simply implored;

SAVE THE CAVIES!

Bobby and Boo held a banner that bore the legend;

SAY <u>NO</u> TO GUINEA PIG GUINEA PIGS!

The press were out in force that day and, fearing bad publicity, Cuthbert Fanshaw reluctantly agreed to stop the testing. While this had improved the image of Fanshaw Cosmetics, it was now far more difficult for the company to develop new products.

Unbeknown to anyone else, Cuthbert Fanshaw had been hatching a plot. Having spoken to his laboratory workers he now called in his two lackeys, Brian Starbuck and Bill Nilly.

'I want you two to find me some animals—about a dozen guinea pigs will do nicely,' he said to them.

'I didn't know you were interested in keeping pets!' grunted Bill.

'They're not *for* pets you imbecile!' boomed Cuthbert.

'Then what *are* they for?' stuttered Brian, a little puzzled.

'They're for testing our products on, isn't that obvious?' rasped Cuthbert impatiently.

'You can't do that!' protested Brian.

'No!' nodded Bill, 'you agreed to stop animal testing!'

'I know I did, but don't you see, it's perfect!' hissed Cuthbert, with a hint of self-satisfaction.

'How's that?' asked Bill and Brian.

'Because if we do the tests in secret no one will suspect us! Everyone knows that we gave all our animals to good homes and now they think we're the good guys.'

'What if someone finds out?' asked Brian warily.

'No one *will* find out if we're very careful, and it's important that you two don't tell anyone what we're up to!' warned Cuthbert sternly. 'Only the laboratory workers know about this and I think they're looking forward to the experiments as much as I am, ha, ha, ha!'

'What about the night-time security guard—do you think you can trust him?' asked Bill.

'Oh yes, I'd forgotten about him—I suppose he'll have to know. Still, I think he needs his job too much!' laughed Cuthbert wickedly.

'Can't you just do tests on rats?—there's plenty of them in the sewers around here!' suggested Brian.

'Ugh, horrible, smelly creatures!—I'd use them as a last resort but right now I prefer to have them working *for* me!'

'Right then, we'll go down to Whitebridge Pet Centre and buy all the guinea pigs they've got!' said Bill.

'*Don't be so stupid!*' roared Cuthbert angrily. 'Hasn't it occurred to you how strange it would look if you just waltzed into a pet shop and bought that many guinea pigs all at once? Anyway, they'll know that you work for me.'

'Oh, I hadn't thought of that,' sighed Bill lamely.

'Well you had better *start* thinking because I want you two to come up with a plan before the day is over!' demanded Cuthbert.

As they were about to leave the room Brian suddenly stopped in his tracks. 'I've had a thought!' he announced.

'Now there's a first, let's declare a public holiday!' bellowed Cuthbert sarcastically.

'About the guinea pigs I mean.'

'Well, go on,' Fanshaw implored him.

'Do you know the Fitchetts at Crickley Meadow?'

'Yes, I know of them—darn troublemakers if I remember rightly,' snarled Cuthbert.

'Well, they've got an outhouse and I've heard it's full of guinea pigs—leastways there's more than a dozen!'

'It sounds perfect!' Cuthbert enthused as he ran over and kissed Brian on the cheek.

'But how will we get them here without anyone knowing?' asked Bill as Brian wiped his cheek with his shirtsleeve.

'We'll kidnap them!' replied Cuthbert.

'Don't you mean *pignap* them,' laughed Brian.

'*I'll* do the jokes thank you very much!' Cuthbert snapped.

'But if we just go in there and take them won't someone suspect?' asked Bill.

'No!' replied Cuthbert smugly, 'and this is the good bit—when you break in just pinch a few garden tools. It will look like an ordinary burglary and then, when they find a few hutches and the garden gate open they'll just think that the stupid creatures have escaped and put themselves at the mercy of the foxes, *ha, ha, ha*!'

'Yes, it sounds like it could work,' Bill surmised

'It *will* work, and I'm relying on you two, so no mistakes!' warned Cuthbert.

'Right, when shall we do it then Cuthy?' asked Brian.

'*Don't call me Cuthy—I'm Mr Fanshaw to you!*' barked Cuthbert.

'Sorry Mr Fanshaw,' winced Brian sheepishly.

'Right well, there's no point in delaying, tonight's as good a time as any!' announced Cuthbert Fanshaw, his lips pursing into a wicked smile.

THE RACE

Mrs Fitchett soon came back into the garden followed by a young girl who was holding a large pet carrier.

'You all know Chloe don't you?—she's going away with her family for the week so she's brought Ted, B1 and B2 and they'll be staying with us until she comes home,' Mrs Fitchett announced. She explained that Chloe's next door neighbour was looking after her two longhaired guinea pigs, Louis and Elvis.

Ted was just a little older than B1 and B2 and was a cute brown rex cavy with a little white patch on his bottom. The *B* in B1 and B2 stood for Babe. They were identical twins with short white fur and red albino eyes and, because they were so alike, Chloe decided to give them the same name but distinguish them with the numbers 1 and 2. Even Chloe was only able to tell which one was which by looking closely at their heads as B1's was very slightly tilted to the right. All of them had met Ted and Bs 1 and 2 before. Ted had come to stay one weekend and had enjoyed it so much that he was extremely excited about coming again. B1 and B2, on the other hand, were somewhat less enthusiastic even though, in a way, they were coming *home*.

Boo had given birth to them at Fernbrook Cottage but they had gone to live with Chloe when they were old enough to leave their mother. Although they were looking forward to seeing Boo again, as well as their sisters Cleo and Flossy, they were not too sure about staying at Fernbrook Cottage all week. The trouble was that they had become a little pampered at Chloe's house where they actually lived indoors, and they felt they would be *roughing it* by living in an outhouse again.

Chloe placed the pet carrier on the lawn and opened the door. Ted sprang out immediately and was greeted by enthusiastic squeaking.

Freddy bounded straight up to him and yelled, 'hey Ted, come and play hide and seek with us,' as he gestured towards Cleo, Flossy and Dorie.

Freddy was excited to know that he wouldn't just be playing with girls all the time.

'Yes, I will,' answered Ted, 'but let's wait for B1 and B2 first.'

B1 and B2 were very slow to come out—almost reluctant you might say—but when they did they enjoyed the enthusiastic welcome that they received and, of course, waiting to greet them was Boo, who came straight over and purred as the three snuggled up together.

Ted realised that there was going to be a bit of a reunion and so he decided to go and play and leave the twins to join in later. The children ran off while Boo went with B1 and B2 to the conifer to catch up on some gossip.

Meanwhile Chloe, who knew all the guinea pigs names, wandered around the garden, greeting them individually and picking up the ones she was able to catch, giving each a little cuddle. When it was time for her to go she bade a fond farewell to them all but especially to Ted, B1 and B2.

'Well, that's it now—we're stuck here,' moaned B1.

'Oh it's not all that bad,' shrugged B2, 'we've been made to feel very welcome and we can have some wonderful games in this garden.'

'Yes, I suppose so,' B1 sighed, 'but just look around you!'

'What do you mean?'

'Well, take those two for example.' B1 was pointing to Badger and Gnasher who were still arguing and had started baring their teeth at each other. 'I mean, can you *believe* their behaviour?—if you ask me they're just *riff raff!*'

'I know what you mean,' agreed B2, 'but I don't think they're as bad as all that, they're just a little high spirited.'

'You can say that again!' replied B1, 'even Chloe's mum said we were going to be living with riff raff!'

'Yes, but she was only joking—I think!' said B2 unconvincingly.

'And what about having to sleep in an *outhouse?*' moaned B1.

'I must admit that I'm not looking forward to that,' B2 nodded.

They both agreed that the week ahead was going to be a long one.

The argument that Badger and Gnasher were having was still raging and was beginning to get on a few nerves. Eventually Rosie approached them.

'Why are you two always arguing?' she asked.

'It's his fault!' they blurted out together.

'Well, if you ask me you're as bad as each other and I think it's about time you sorted out your differences and gave the rest of us a bit of peace,' snapped Rosie. 'Now tell me what the row is about this time.'

'Well *he* said…!' they replied in unison once again.

'Now *stop*,' commanded Rosie firmly, 'you can tell me one at a time, starting with Badger.'

They might spend all their time arguing with each other but neither Badger nor Gnasher was going to mess with Rosie in this mood.

Badger began. 'Well it all started when I told Gnasher that I could run faster than him but he just wouldn't have it.'

'No, that's because I can run faster than you!' Gnasher protested.

'Oh shut up big nose!' was Badger's unkind repost.

'I'm sick of you poking fun at my hooter!' roared Gnasher as he squared up to Badger.

'*Boys, boys, boys!*' admonished Rosie, each word increasing in crescendo. 'This just won't do—you've got to put a stop to all this nonsense and I think I know a way we can settle this argument once and for all—now listen to me!'

Badger and Gnasher both fell silent for once as they waited for Rosie to continue.

'I've decided that you're going to have a race!'

'*A race?*' they exclaimed in surprise.

'Yes, that's right, a race! It's better than fighting and, as for which one of you can run the fastest, it will settle the argument once and for all!'

The boys shrugged their shoulders in resignation as Rosie busied herself with working out the layout of the course. She then appointed some of the girls to steward parts of the track. Their job would be to make sure that the contestants ran round them and did not take any short cuts. The race was to consist of one lap of the garden in a clockwise direction, beginning and ending by the outdoor hutch.

'That means I'll get a grandstand view of the finish,' beamed Sniffer.

'You will that,' smiled Rosie, 'but not from the comfort of the hutch—we need a finishing line and you're going to be holding the string with me! That reminds me—have we got any string?'

'Now that's a point,' Smokey frowned.

'*I know—I've seen some string!*' shouted Freddy excitedly, 'it's over by Harold!'

They were wondering what Freddy meant as he headed for the conifer at the opposite end of the row of trees to *Cuddles* but he soon returned with a piece of string.

'I don't think that's going to be long enough,' groaned Gracie, as Freddy's feeling of being the hero of the hour quickly evaporated.

'There's another piece like that over here,' yelled Flossy who was standing by Sniffer's Rock.

'If we could tie the two together it would be long enough,' said Rosie. 'Can anyone tie knots?' she called out.

They all looked at each other but no one came forward to claim that they possessed this particular skill.

B1 had been observing all the events connected with the organisation of the race but had managed to ensure that her veneer of feigned boredom did not crack.

After this latest episode she just looked at B2 and shook her head. 'Can you believe that?—thirty of them and not one can tie a knot!'

'It's not their fault—they're not educated like us!' said B2.

'Shall we go and help out then?' suggested B1.

'Yes, come on!'

The pair came and took a piece of string each and B1 placed one end on the ground. Then B2 took one end of her piece in her mouth and crossed it over the other piece and cleverly looped it round. She held it there while B1 looped the end of her piece back round B2's, then both of them pulled together and, *hey presto!*—they had a knot. Now there was a piece of string long enough for the finishing line.

The males had hitherto taken little interest in all the kerfuffle surrounding the race but now that it was nearly ready to begin, Cedric had suggested that they should take bets on the outcome.

'Hey, that sounds like a great idea,' enthused Charlie.

'It all sounds very good,' Bobby cut in, 'but what are we going to bet with?'

Dylan agreed. 'That's a good point, none of us owns anything!'

'Cedric owns something,' said Patrick.

They all looked at him a little puzzled before he added—'his cigarettes!'

'You can forget that, I'm not gambling with them,' protested Cedric.

'I shouldn't worry, I'm sure none of us would want to win them anyway,' grunted Cyril.

'Let's just do it for *cavy honour* then,' suggested Bobby.

'What do you mean?' asked Patrick.

'We just divide ourselves into teams—those who support Badger and those who support Gnasher.'

'That's good,' nodded Patrick, 'and those in the winning team can bask in the reflected glory.'

'What about the losers?' asked Charlie.

'They'll just have to be phil…phil whassisname about it,' stuttered Patrick.

'Who's Phil whassisname?' Cedric asked.

'I think he means philosophical,' said Dylan.

'Phil O'Sophical—is he one of your Irish friends Patrick?' Charlie enquired.

'Right!' exclaimed Cedric, 'I'm up for Gnasher!'

'Me too!' agreed Charlie.

Patrick also pledged his support for Gnasher while Bobby, Dylan and Cyril all agreed that they were going to be supporting Badger. All those involved in stewarding the race had to be strictly impartial and the children were either too excited or, in B1 and B2's case, too disinterested to care. Of the remaining eleven girls, Jessie said she did not want to get over-excited but would support Badger. Pauline, Monica, Boo, Mandy and Gracie did likewise, while Maisie, Joey, Emily, Miffy and Buttons were going to root for Gnasher.

'Are you boys ready?' Rosie asked.

They both agreed that they were about as ready as they'd ever be and so Rosie explained to them how she was going to begin the race and warned, *'no false starts!'*

All the stewards were in their places and the *spectators* were in various positions but none were too far from the start/finish line. Freddy, Dorie and Ted were standing behind Badger and Gnasher as they intended to run with them and see if they could keep up.

Everyone went quiet and as the tension started to grow, Rosie gave the order, 'take your marks!' to which the contestants lined up behind the string that had been laid on the ground. Then she called out, 'get set!' to which Badger and Gnasher wound themselves up ready—*'go!'*

The boys sprang off together and headed side by side towards Sniffer's Rock. There was nothing between them as they turned right along the path towards the outhouse door.

'Come on, we can catch them,' shouted Freddy to Ted as they passed Sniffer's Rock. Dorie had dropped out already!

'Do you really think so?' asked Ted doubtfully, as they turned right and saw Badger and Gnasher way ahead running past Misty at the steps to the outhouse door.

Ted dropped out before reaching Misty and by the time Freddy reached her, Badger and Gnasher were already running past Smokey at the corner of the patio and doubling back towards the fishpond. Freddy continued for a while but stopped short of Smokey, completely out of breath.

By this time, the official contestants were dashing past Lucky and round the pond virtually neck-and-neck, as they had been for the whole of the race so far. Both of them had got slightly in the lead once or twice but the other would always catch up. As they headed towards Sandy at the far end of the pond Gnasher decided to indulge in a bit of gamesmanship.

'This isn't the fastest you can run is it Badger?—I've barely got going yet!'

Badger glanced at him but decided to ignore Gnasher and concentrate his efforts on running.

Once past Sandy they hurtled towards the greenhouse, vanishing out of view for a few seconds as they ran round it. When they emerged they were heading towards where most of the onlookers were now standing. The tension was building and the *crowd* was starting to get vociferous. There were shouts of encouragement for both of the contestants.

'Come on Badger!' chanted a group of the girls.

'Come on Gnasher—there's honour at stake!' bellowed Patrick.

Still there was nothing between them. Badger would find an extra stride from somewhere but when he did, Gnasher would match him.

'It could be a tie at this rate,' suggested Cedric.

'*Honours even* wouldn't be too bad a result!' stated Patrick.

Badger and Gnasher were now striding with such vicious determination towards the bottom corner of the garden that Tufty was fearful of getting bowled over. With the cheering building up, they approached the corner still side by side, but Badger was canny enough to have made sure he was on the inside as they rounded Tufty. Rosie and Sniffer were now holding the string tight at the finishing line and all the spectators had gathered round them, trying to get a bird's-eye view.

Now on the final straight, the contestants could both see the string that Sniffer and Rosie were pulling taut. They made a last valiant effort to reach it first and with only yards to go Badger was in the lead by about three inches. This made Gnasher determined to run faster than he had ever done in his life and, with the cheering now almost deafening, he managed to catch up with Badger. As they reached the finishing line they were once again neck-and-neck but it was Gnasher who had won the race by a nose, as it was this part of his anatomy that made first contact with the string.

Huge cheers went up from Gnasher's supporters and many of them went over to congratulate him.

'What did I tell you?' beamed Cedric to Charlie and Patrick.

'Yes, well done Gnasher, and hooray for that hooter of yours!' cheered Patrick. 'Did they make you bionic when they operated on you that time?' he enquired in jest.

Sniffer had jumped straight back into the hutch to find that Jessie was in a little pain and distress.

'I think I might be starting,' she said to Sniffer.

'Snff, just sit there, I'm sure you'll be alright. When Mrs Fitchett comes out she'll have you straight inside and into the maternity hutch—now don't worry about anything, snff.'

Sniffer was so reassuring that Jessie immediately calmed down and relaxed.

Outside the hutch, the furore was just beginning to die down. While Gnasher had been enjoying his victory and all the congratulations that went with it, Badger had got away from everyone. He was very tired after putting everything into the race and very dejected at losing so narrowly.

Bobby had noticed him and had come over to offer his commiserations.

'You raced brilliantly,' he said.

'Not brilliantly enough to win though, and now Gnasher will never let me forget that he beat me.'

'He shouldn't be too hard on you, you raced just as well as he did and, let's face it, he only won because of the size of his nose!'

'Maybe, but I don't think he'll see it that way,' Badger moaned.

'Well let's just hope that he doesn't get too carried away with it all.' replied Bobby.

It was now early evening and it wouldn't be long before the Fitchetts came out to get them all back in their hutches. Jessie was still quite calm but a little worried as she didn't fancy having her litter in the outdoor hutch. Most of the others had gone back into their huddles and were either just sitting down or chewing some grass. It had been a long day and they were all very tired. Even the children had stopped playing and were sitting with the grown-ups. Badger was still sitting alone, not too far from the outhouse door, as all he wanted to do was go back in.

Gnasher was over by Sniffer's Rock and had been thinking about the race ever since the congratulations had died down. He felt very proud to have won but after a while had begun thinking about what it must have been like to lose, especially with it being so close. He ambled over to Badger.

'I suppose you've come to gloat—well you've got every right to— after all you did win,' grunted Badger.

'Some of them are saying that I only won because of the size of my nose but let's face it, I did win fair and square!'

'I can't really argue with that, but I bet I could beat you in a fight!' asserted Badger, desperate to cling on to some pride.

'We'll have to see about that won't we?' Gnasher replied.

He was not going to give any quarter to Badger, especially given the exultation he felt at having won the race.

'Maybe we *will see about that* and it can't come quickly enough as far as I'm concerned!' Badger stated defiantly.

The pair had now become so weary that the arguing stopped and they just sat there not speaking or moving.

The Fitchetts came out soon afterwards and Mrs Fitchett immediately noticed Badger and Gnasher sitting together.

'Look at that!' she exclaimed to Mr Fitchett.

'They appear to be getting on with each other—now there's a turn up for the books!' Mr Fitchett replied.

The Fitchetts cautiously approached the boys fully expecting them to run away but to their surprise, found that they were able to catch them quite easily.

'You two are usually the last to be caught,' said Mrs Fitchett.

Most of the others were getting ready to play *catch us if you can*.

'Are you getting ready to run when the Fitchetts try and catch you?' Freddy asked Ted.

'You bet,' replied Ted.

'Why bother?' grunted B1.

'Yes, what's the point?' moaned B2.

'The point is that it's good fun and the last one to be caught is the winner for the day,' explained Freddy.

'And we've got a good chance tonight now that Badger and Gnasher are already in,' nodded Rosie.

'Also, we have to play for the Fitchetts sake,' said Emily.

'Why?' B1 asked, bewildered.

'Because they love playing and they'd be very disappointed if we didn't play along,' affirmed Rosie.

'Rubbish! We're not going to bother playing are we B2?' frowned B1.

'No way!' bleated B2.

The Fitchetts emerged from the outhouse looking for the *easiest* targets first. They went to get Sniffer but Mrs Fitchett noticed Jessie.

'I'm taking her indoors—she can stay there until she's had her babies.'

Mr Fitchett grabbed Sniffer without any trouble but the rest of them were not so easy to catch. Smokey always used to be one of the first back in but had recently started to learn some of the tricks of the game and she'd even managed to win on two occasions. However, she was very tired tonight and was in next.

Mrs Fitchett was back out now and, one by one, they started to be brought in. Some of them were naïve in their tactics and would hide behind a rock or the outdoor hutch only to find their way blocked at both ends, while others would run away from one of their pursuers only to run straight into the hands of the other.

After twenty minutes there were only six of them left. Surprisingly, B1 and B2 were still there as were Monica, Buttons, Emily and Cedric. Cedric was not as fast as most of the others but made up for this by finding clever places to hide.

'It's going to be a girl winner tonight,' smiled Emily.

'Not if I've got anything to do with it,' said Cedric.

Emily rounded on B1 and B2. 'Anyway, I thought you two weren't playing!'

Before the twins could answer, a pair of hands grabbed the off-guard B1 from behind as the other girls scrambled away. Buttons and Monica headed straight under the bush but it was immediately surrounded and, after a short game of *cat and mouse*, they were back in the outhouse. Cedric was hiding under a plant by the fishpond, thinking that they'd never find him there. Mr Fitchett walked towards the greenhouse then suddenly pounced on a surprised Cedric, ensuring a *girly* victory.

Both pursuers approached the outdoor hutch together and lifted it up suddenly to reveal a surprised Emily. As Mr Fitchett tried to grab her she turned and ran, but only into the hands of Mrs Fitchett. B2 was the winner and only showed token resistance before being shown to the temporary quarters she was to share with B1.

After they'd been fed and had their hay and water replenished, Mrs Fitchett turned off the outhouse lights, locked the door and suggested to Mr Fitchett that they go and see how Jessie was getting on.

All was silent and still in the outhouse now. It had been an eventful day and they were all exhausted, even Sniffer, although he was admittedly concerned about Jessie. Badger and Gnasher had been resting since being brought in while B1, and especially B2, were feeling a little *chuffed* at their success in the game of *catch us if you can*.

The other children were all flat-out and Cedric didn't even bother to smoke the last cigarette that he usually had at bedtime, much to the relief of Cyril. They all just wanted to lie down and rest their weary bodies and they definitely did not want any more excitement. Such was the scene of serenity and calmness that presented itself in the outhouse as the light of day gradually faded from the window to be replaced by the mellow glow of the full moon.

CHAPTER FIVE

AN UNEXPECTED TURN OF EVENTS

It was about 3.30am and all was peaceful. Brian Starbuck and Bill Nilly parked their van just beyond the end of the Fernbrook Cottage driveway and, aided by the moonlight, made their way round to the fields at the rear. They scaled the garden fence and, armed with a crowbar, a torch and a canvas sack, approached the outhouse.

The crack of the padlock being wrenched off the outhouse door startled all the animals and also worried the intruders, who were concerned that the noise might be heard from the cottage. They waited for a short while to ensure that nobody stirred and, once they felt it was safe, entered the building.

The guinea pigs sensed that something was amiss and the cacophonous squeaking that resulted unsettled Brian and Bill.

'Shut up you blasted lot!' hissed Brian, as he shone his torch towards the source of the noise.

'You look a likely bunch—I think Mr Fanshaw will like you!' enthused Bill, as, sack in hand, he moved towards Pauline's hutch and opened the door.

The girl's cowered in the corner as Bill's large hand reached in to grab them. After a short struggle all four were in the sack but not before Bill had received a sharp nip from both Pauline and Tufty.

'*Come on, come on, hurry up!*' frowned Brian nervously as he shone the torch.

'Ah—over there!' pointed Bill as he opened two adjacent hutches and grabbed Boo, Joey, Emily, Cleo and Flossy, leaving behind the remaining youngsters in the open hutch.

Bill counted his fingers. 'That's nine, now we want another…?'

'Three,' interjected Brian.

By now, Bill was rushing and was just opening hutches and grabbing whom he could. He opened Badger's hutch and then Gnasher's but they gnashed and bit so fiercely that he gave up on them. He then tried to grab Sniffer who was so determined to evade capture that he wriggled free and fell to the floor. Sandy, Smokey, Cyril, and Dylan were soon ensnared and thrown into the sack.

'That's thirteen now,' announced Bill

'We've got an extra one for luck then,' replied Brian.

'I thought thirteen was supposed to be *unlucky*,' Bill grimaced as he pulled the sack over his shoulder.

At that the intruders quickly left, Brian remembering to grab a spade and a lawnmower as he went. This time they departed through a gate, deliberately leaving it open, before running to their van, throwing the *loot* in the back and making off towards Whitebridge.

Badger and Gnasher, whose hutches had been left open, jumped to the floor from a height of about four feet, managing to fall without hurting themselves. They joined Cedric, Bobby and Sniffer.

'What are we going to do now?' sighed Sniffer.

'What *can* we do?' shrugged Gnasher in resignation.

'We can go and look for them,' suggested Bobby.

'How are we going to do that?—they could be anywhere?' groaned Badger.

Bobby had been alerted by something that Bill Nilly had said. 'They could be, but I strongly suspect they're going to be at Fanshaw's laboratory on the other side of Whitebridge.'

'That's right, one of those men mentioned Mr Fanshaw—that must be where they're taking them,' agreed Cedric.

'Don't you think we should just stay here and get a good night's rest and let the Fitchetts sort it out tomorrow?' grumbled Sniffer.

'The Fitchetts won't know that it's Fanshaw and they'll just put us back in our hutches,' Bobby replied.

'So, if we are going to go and look for them it will have to be now!' nodded Badger, the implications having dawned upon him.

'If you're to be goin' anywhere then we're coming too,' shouted Patrick from a hutch also about four feet above. The hutch had been opened in the melee but the occupants had managed to avoid being caught.

'I don't think we'll be able to get down there,' Charlie frowned.

'It's easy, I saw Badger and Gnasher do it before—watch me!' boasted Patrick as he leapt out of the open door and landed heavily on his four paws.

'Are you alright Patrick?' asked Cedric.

'Yes, oi'll be fine!' Patrick assured him as he shook his front paws to ease the pain.

'If *you* can do it then so can I!' insisted Charlie as he lunged towards the doorway.

'No wait!' shouted Patrick, fearing that Charlie might do himself some serious damage.

But Charlie was already on his way down, landing on his bottom and rolling over a couple of times before coming to rest on his side.

'Oh no—Ch...*Charlie!*' stammered Patrick in a state of panic.

'I'm fine, just a bit of bruising to the rear,' Charlie assured Patrick as he sat up and placed his trilby back on his head.

'Let's get on our way then,' commanded Bobby.

'You're not going anywhere without us,' protested B1, *us* meaning herself, B2 and Ted.

'You're too young and anyway, you're hutch is still closed,' Bobby pointed out.

'Maybe we can get you out,' cried Freddy as he ran up with Dorie alongside him.

They had hidden when their ground floor hutch was opened and had now reappeared. As Bobby protested, B1 was directing Freddy to a stick in the corner of the outhouse which he duly fetched. Upon further instruction, Dorie climbed on Freddy's back and directed the stick towards the knob that kept the hutch locked. She was soon able to turn it and in no time its three occupants had joined the others, making the number of pursuers up to twelve.

'I'm really not sure you children should be coming with us on such a dangerous mission,' Bobby argued.

'I'm not too sure about it either,' confided Dorie to Freddy as she recalled the conversation from the previous day about the world beyond the fence.

'We mustn't be afraid of *anything*—we've *got* to try and rescue mum and Aunty Joey if we can,' Freddy insisted.

'Before we go anywhere, do we know where this Fanshaw place is?' asked B1 sensibly.

Bobby, who was by now assuming control of the operation, answered her.

'All I know is that it's on the other side of Whitebridge. We know that Whitebridge is directly away to the back of here and if we keep going we must surely find it.'

'And when we get to Whitebridge maybe someone will find us and take us to Fanshaw's place,' suggested Badger.

'When we get to Whitebridge we mustn't let anybody find us because if they do catch us they'll bring us back here, and then who's going to rescue our friends?' frowned Bobby before authoritatively giving the direction, 'right—let's get going!'

'Be careful won't you?' shouted Miffy as the cavies who were going to be left behind looked on forlornly from their hutches.

'Look after yourself and come back soon Cedric,' cried Misty.

'How are we going to get out of the garden,' pondered Cedric, remembering that all the exits were blocked.

'Silly us for not thinking of that,' groaned Bobby.

'Let's go and look—maybe they left a gate open,' suggested Patrick.

'Yes, come on!' instructed Bobby.

They all quickly left the outhouse through the door left open by the intruders. Gnasher was the first down the step and noticed that the gate was still open and he waited for the rest to clamber down.

'That's a bit of luck to find the gate op...!' Bobby faltered because at that second there was a gentle gust of wind and the gate slammed shut before any of them could reach it.

'Well, that's it now,' B1 grunted.

'Snff, oh well, we might as well go back to our hutches,' beamed Sniffer.

'We're not going back anywhere,' Bobby declared sternly.

'But...!' Sniffer started to mutter in protestation.

Bobby was uncompromising. 'There are no *buts*—we're going to get out of here even if we have to fly out!'

'You must be joking, only birds and winged insects can fly,' laughed Badger.

'People can fly,' affirmed B1.

'That's right, they've even flown to that round thing up there,' nodded B2.

'You mean the moon?' queried Dorie. 'How can anyone fly up *there*? I mean, it must be at least a mile away!'

'It's a bit further than that and people *have* flown there,' B1 assured her.

'Beats me how anyone can fly all that way!' Patrick sighed.

'It's easy—you just need a space rocket,' B1 informed him.

'You seem to know a lot about it,' probed Gnasher.

'Well, the thing is, we're *educated*,' stated B2 aloofly.

'Oh really, and where exactly did you acquire this education of yours?' asked Patrick.

B2 whispered to B1 to ask her what *acquire* meant before answering.

'Er—well, Chloe's got a lot of books you know!'

'Do you *really* read books?' Gnasher pressed.

'And there are some very informative programmes on the television too!' B2 spluttered, ignoring Gnasher's question.

'So that's it!—they get their education from watching the telly!' declared Patrick.

'Well we do watch the odd program,' admitted B1.

'I suppose *you* two are so clever that you could even build a space rocket yourselves!' Charlie sarcastically goaded the twins.

'Yes, as a matter of fact we could,' scowled B1 defiantly.

'Oh yeah, how?' demanded Cedric.

'It's easy—all we need is an empty washing-up liquid bottle, a piece of cardboard, a pair of scissors and some sticky tape!' pronounced B1, as B2 nodded in agreement.

'No doubt you learned that from the telly too!' teased Patrick.

'Yes, we did actually!' bleated the twins.

Bobby was beginning to lose patience. 'Come on now, this isn't getting us anywhere—there has to be a way out of here and we're going to find it!'

'There's only one way out of here and that's by shifting Sniffer's Rock,' Patrick groaned.

'We may as well give up then,' shrugged Freddy as he remembered his vain efforts of the previous day.

'Maybe if we all pushed together we could do it,' suggested Bobby.

Badger was not convinced. 'I'm not even sure that would work.'

'Well, it's got to be worth a try,' protested Gnasher.

'Gnasher's quite right, we must at least try it,' agreed Bobby.

Bobby then proceeded to organise everyone so that they were in the best possible position to get their weight behind the rock. He put himself, Charlie and Patrick at the front, pushing directly on the rock, with Cedric, Badger and Gnasher pushing them from behind. Behind them were Sniffer, Ted, Freddy and Dorie although B1 and B2 refused to join in as they considered the whole exercise to be futile.

When they were all in position Bobby declared, 'right, I'm going to count to three and then we all push together—ok?'

'What does three come after?' asked Patrick.

'Right, I'm going to say *one, two, three* and then we all push, so are we ready?' Bobby took the silence that greeted him as a yes and then cried, 'one, two, three—*push!*'

They pushed together with all their might but the rock did not budge.

'It's hopeless,' moaned Badger.

'We'll give it one more try,' insisted Bobby.

Again he counted and they pushed with all the strength they could muster but the rock remained steadfast.

'You're right,' agreed Bobby, 'it's not going to shift.'

'So what do we do now?' asked Charlie.

'Don't say we didn't tell you,' B1 arrogantly boasted, much to Patrick's annoyance.

'If you two had joined in it might have made the difference,' he fired back, irritated by B1's *know it all* attitude.

'Come on, give them a break,' implored Ted, 'after all they *were* right and we know it wouldn't have made a difference anyway.'

'Maybe not, but perhaps *you* two can come up with a bright idea,' Patrick challenged the twins.

'Perhaps we can!' blurted B1.

Remembering a science programme he had seen recently on the television, Ted suddenly declared that he'd had an idea. He explained that they needed a strong stick made of wood or metal, one end of which they would place under the rock with the middle being raised by another smaller rock. Then, if enough of them could put their weight on the other end of the stick, they could lever the rock upwards.

'Yes, of course,' nodded B1, 'actually, I was just about to think of that!'

'Well, what are we waiting for?—let's find a suitable stick!' yelled Patrick.

'How about this one?' asked Gnasher, pointing to a piece of cane that was lying close by.

'That won't be strong enough,' sighed Ted.

'This one might do,' suggested Sniffer.

He pointed out a piece of timber about two feet long and about an inch by half an inch thick that was lying on the ground near the outhouse.

'I think that *will* do it!' enthused Ted.

'Now all we need is a small rock,' added B1.

With Ted and B1 supervising, they soon found a broken piece of brick near the fence and nudged it into position. They then managed to lift the timber onto the brick, pushing one end of it into place at the bottom of Sniffer's Rock and wedging it underneath.

All they needed to do now was to put all their weight on the other end. The problem was that it was quite high up. B1 decided that Badger and Gnasher should climb up first with Bobby, Cedric, Charlie and Patrick after them. It was a difficult balancing act with Badger and Gnasher being underneath the others but when Patrick climbed on top their combined weight did not move the rock.

'That's it then—we might as well give up!' grunted Patrick.

'Don't throw in the towel yet boys!' implored B1.

Remembering how Patrick and Charlie had jumped out of their hutches a little while before, B1 struck on the idea that if the two of them could jump onto the end of the timber from a high enough vantage point, the extra force might just be enough to move the rock. The problem was that there was nowhere to jump from and there ensued a brief discussion between Ted, B1 and B2.

'Right,' declared B1, 'we're going to form a *cavy tower* and Charlie and Patrick will jump from the top of that!'

'What's a cavy tower?' asked Badger.

'I don't know but I don't like the sound of it,' groaned Gnasher.

B1 informed them that, propped against the fence, they were going to climb on top of each other. Charlie and Patrick suggested that Badger and Gnasher should do the jumping but B1 had other ideas. As Gnasher had feared, he and Badger were going to be at the bottom of the tower with Cedric, Bobby, Sniffer, Ted, Freddy, Dorie, B2 and B1, in that order, climbing above them. Lastly, Charlie and Patrick would climb to the top and jump off together, landing on the end of the timber.

The tower was duly formed with poor Badger and Gnasher taking all the weight at the bottom while the younger ones clung on gingerly at the top. It was difficult for Charlie and Patrick to reach the top because they were not as agile as their smaller compatriots. They clambered up very slowly but were being urged to hurry up by most of the others. Eventually they reached the top and, with Charlie standing on the shoulders of B1 and Patrick slightly below him with one foot on B2's back, they held paws and looked down.

'I can't do it!' declared Charlie.

'Of course you can!' cried Patrick who lurched forward, pulling Charlie with him.

Patrick landed right on target in a sitting position with Charlie near enough on his lap. As they landed they felt the timber giving way and instinctively thought it was going to snap. However, it held firm and, to the astonishment and relief of them all, except perhaps Sniffer, the other end levered the rock upwards and sideways. Charlie and Patrick fell off and the *cavy tower* dismantled itself slowly from the top down.

'Anything broken?' Charlie enquired of Patrick.

'I don't think so but I think you've lost something,' Patrick replied.

'If you're referring to my will to live you could be right!'

'No, I mean your hat!' chuckled Patrick as he returned it to Charlie who then placed it on his head once more.

Ted ran straight to the gap between the rock and the fence to see if it was big enough to get through.

'Us smaller ones will be ok but I'm not sure about some of you bigger guys,' was Ted's verdict.

'What if we can't get through—what's going to happen then?' asked Cedric.

'We'll have to try the *cavy tower* again,' replied Ted.

'*Oh no we won't!*' cried Patrick, Charlie, Badger, Gnasher, Cedric, Bobby and Sniffer as one voice.

The younger ones all went out through the gap, followed one by one by the adults. Badger was lithe enough to squeeze through without too much trouble and Sniffer soon followed him. Gnasher decided to wait till last in case any pushing was needed. Patrick was able to get through the gap but his bruises made the experience a painful one. Charlie was able to do likewise and Bobby got through more easily than expected due to the fact that his long hair gave him the appearance of being bigger than he actually was.

'Cedric won't have any trouble then,' Freddy mused, but as Cedric's head appeared through the gap the rest of him did not follow.

'Cedric must be as fat as he looks,' sniggered B1 to B2.

'I think I'll have to give up and let you all go without me,' grunted Cedric.

'*Oh no you won't!*' protested Bobby who got ready to pull one paw and told Badger to get ready to pull the other. Bobby then shouted over to Gnasher, '*push when I say so.*'

On the command, Bobby and Badger both pulled Cedric while Gnasher pushed him from the rear. Dorie and Freddy thought the eyes were going to pop out of Cedric's head as he moved further through the gap but still he wasn't through.

'I don't think I'll be going forwards or backwards now,' moaned Cedric.

'*Oh yes you will!*' cried Bobby who urged Badger and Gnasher on to one more valiant effort. The eyes nearly *did* pop out of Cedric's head this time as he was pulled and pushed until he suddenly exploded through the gap, flattening Bobby and Badger in the process. Cedric slowly pulled himself up and then suddenly remembered the last cigarette that he had left in his hutch and announced that he would have to go back for it.

'*Oh no you won't!*' declared the rest of them and Cedric ruefully gave it up as a bad idea.

As Gnasher crawled through to join the others in the field, the time was approaching 5.00am and it was beginning to get light.

'Well done everybody!' said Patrick.

'Yes, we've all done very well so far but now the real adventure begins!' added Bobby as he looked out across the field towards the distant horizon.

CHAPTER SIX

DANGER ON THE ROAD TO WHITEBRIDGE

Bobby decided that there was no time to lose and urged the group to start making their way across the field. They set off over the uneven surface of ploughed soil with Badger and Gnasher trying to set a fast pace, though soon realising that they would need to adjust their speed to suit everyone else. The youngsters started quickly enough but it was not long before they began to tire and were forced to slow down. The slowest, however, was Cedric who soon found himself short of breath and was suggesting that they stop for a rest barely halfway across the first field.

'You must be joking—it'll take us two months to get to Whitebridge if we're to be stoppin' every five minutes!' Patrick protested.

'I'm sorry people,' shrugged Cedric, wheezing, 'but it's my chest, I think I need a cigarette.'

'I've never heard anything so ridiculous in my life!' snapped Charlie.

Bobby informed Cedric that they would have a rest but not before they had put a bit of distance between them and Crickley Meadow *and* found something to eat and drink. They continued on their way and reached the other side of the field about half an hour after setting off. There were grass verges at the edge, upon which they briefly chewed, before clambering through the hedgerow towards the next field.

They started out across it, weaving between the stubble of harvested wheat with Badger and Gnasher the pacesetters once again. The stubble was taller than *they* were and it would be very easy for any of them to get lost, so they needed to ensure that they stayed close together. Bobby, Badger or Gnasher would stretch their necks periodically in order to check that they were still going in the right direction.

'I do hope we can rest up soon,' Cedric moaned to Sniffer as they walked together at the back.

'I do too; snff, to tell you the truth I'd give anything to be sat cosily in my hutch right now and to know how Jessie was doing but I realise that we've got to go on because we're the only hope that our poor captured friends have got,' replied Sniffer.

'That's a very good point Sniffer and I know we must continue,' Cedric managed to say before he began coughing and spluttering. 'I just wish I knew why my chest is so bad.'

Sniffer diplomatically refrained from stating the obvious and the pair continued walking quietly behind the others.

'Not too far now till we reach those trees at the end of this field!' said Badger.

The young ones were very relieved to hear that, as were Cedric and Sniffer. They had been excited enough at the beginning but their enthusiasm was on the wane now and their energy levels likewise. B1 and B2 were as tired as any of them although they tried to keep up their appearance of *unflappability*.

'We won't be stopping at the end of this field will we?' asked B1 even though she secretly longed to do so.

'We shall see,' replied Bobby, who paused before continuing, 'if we can find a stream to drink from we'll stop for a while but, if not, we shall have to press on further.'

'Will we be able to eat anything other than grass?' Dorie asked.

'We might find some dandelions and who knows what else if we're lucky,' answered Bobby.

'I hope we find some water, I'm absolutely parched,' grumbled Freddy.

The sun was low in the sky to their right and in front of them loomed a row of trees.

'Look at that will ya,' enthused Patrick to Charlie, 'It's like one of those oa, oas…!'

'I think you mean oasis,' cut in B1.

'I just hope we find water there,' grunted Charlie.

They came to the end of the stubble and clambered down towards a ditch with trees on either side of it.

'Wait a minute, where's Dorie?' asked Freddy as he suddenly realised that she had not emerged from the stubble with the rest of them.

They all shouted out to her but before Dorie had the chance to answer, something large swooped down from the sky, momentarily disappearing into the stubble before flying skyward again and readying itself for a second assault.

'I've got a feeling that Dorie's exactly at the point where that bird flew into the grass,' shouted Bobby.

'That was a sparrowhawk and it will come back for her again,' screeched B2.

'Let's get in there quick!' screamed Gnasher as he and Badger, followed by the rest, launched themselves to the rescue.

As swift as they were, they could not reach Dorie before the sparrowhawk and this time it had managed to get her in its claws and lift her skywards.

'No you don't!' cried Gnasher, grabbing Dorie's hind paws in the nick of time.

A *tug-of-war* ensued between Gnasher and the sparrowhawk, until Badger managed to leap high enough to ensnare the bird's tail in his teeth and drag it towards the ground. In fear, the sparrowhawk released Dorie, whereupon Badger set the bird free and watched it soar away.

There was much concern for Dorie's well being. She was extremely shaken and had sustained a slightly torn ear in the tussle. They all stayed very close together as Dorie was led to the ditch at the edge of the field.

'We have to be more careful from now on and never leave anyone alone,' commanded Bobby.

'It doesn't bear thinking about what might have happened to poor young Dorie,' Cedric frowned.

'Anyway, there's no water here!' proclaimed Patrick, who had taken it upon himself to investigate.

They decided to press on and they made their way through the trees. Badger was ahead of the group when he came across a rather large creature with a long black and white nose.

'What are you?' the creature asked Badger, never having encountered a guinea pig before.

'I'm a guinea pig and my name's Badger—what are you?'

'I'm a badger but my name isn't guinea pig,' laughed the nocturnal creature.

'What is your name then?' asked Dorie who, along with the rest of the group, had now caught up.

'My name is Norris and it's nice to meet all you...er...guinea pigs I'm sure, but I really must be getting on because there will be people around here soon,' he insisted.

'What's wrong with people?' B2 enquired.

'Never trust them—steer clear of people. That advice has been handed down from my forefathers,' replied Norris.

'We think people are alright, they look after us,' stated Cedric.

'Really?' Norris sounded genuinely surprised.

'There are some nasty ones though, like those men who broke into the outhouse,' Freddy reminded Cedric.

'And Cuthbert Fanshaw,' added Patrick.

'Don't forget Kurt Sting!' interjected Dorie.

'What's Kurt Sting?' Norris asked.

'*Who's* Kurt Sting?' the guinea pigs corrected Norris, before he shuffled off insisting it was time to go. He bade them farewell but added a stark warning.

'Keep a look out for Danny Fox!'

'Goodbye Badger Norris,' shouted Dorie after him as he swiftly disappeared.

'How many fathers did Norris say he had?' Dorie asked B2.

'Four!'

'So, if his fathers had four fathers as well, how many grandfathers has he got? Dorie enquired further.

B2 replied; 'er, four times four, um that's um—quite a lot!'

'Wow!' exclaimed Dorie, 'imagine trying to remember all their birthdays!'

'Does Whitebridge ever get any nearer?' moaned Charlie, but no one answered as they trundled once again over lumpy soil, ascending gently uphill towards a row of trees now visible on the horizon.

After a while another group of buildings came into view over to the left.

'What town's that then?' asked Patrick.

'That's not a town, silly—that's a farm,' replied B2.

'Oh yes, of course,' Patrick muttered.

Cedric and Sniffer again brought up the rear and Cedric complained, 'this is getting harder than ever—still I'm not going to grumble!'

Just then a large creature that they at first mistook for a dog came into view close by on their right hand side. They soon realised that it wasn't a dog at all but a fox that was out looking for its supper before retiring for the day. The guinea pigs froze as the fox spotted them from about ten yards away and now they remembered Norris's unheeded warning.

'Well what have we got here?—it looks like I've got a choice of menu this morning!' laughed the fearsome looking creature.

Danny Fox was hissing, 'now, do I go for small and succulent or big and filling?' as he eyed up the delightful array that stood before him.

The guinea pigs, particularly the young ones, were understandably terrified, especially Dorie, for whom the sparrowhawk episode was all too fresh in her mind.

'Now you look very tasty to me,' snarled the fox as he looked in the direction of B1.

'You'll have to get past us first!' insisted Badger, as he and Gnasher stepped forward, followed by Bobby, Patrick and Charlie.

None of them had ever felt so frightened in their lives but they realised that they would have to do something if all their companions, especially poor old B1, were going to survive this latest ordeal.

'Oh, so gallant,' mocked Danny Fox before continuing, 'but I can take all of you if I choose, so why don't you just leave the little white one to me and I'll let the rest of you go!'

'Then you'll have to *try* and take all of us!' growled Gnasher defiantly as Cedric, Sniffer, Freddy and Ted all moved forward now as well.

'Very well, have it your way you fools—at least you won't live to regret it!' laughed Danny Fox as he started edging towards them.

There was no time for discussions or planning—they had to act on instinct if they were to have any chance of defying Danny Fox. Acting on instinct was what Badger and Gnasher did best. However it was B2 who made the first move in a desperate attempt to save her sister.

'Catch me if you can you big bully!' she shouted as she started to run away.

'I don't think that will be too difficult!' the fox replied as he bounded towards B2, catching her in his teeth in one swift movement.

'Oh no!' screeched B1 as her poor sister squealed helplessly in the sharp jaws of the sly creature.

Badger and Gnasher reacted instantaneously, running towards Danny at full tilt, Badger leaping and crashing into his hind end while Gnasher careered into his head. Taken aback, Danny dropped B2 but swiftly rounded on his attackers.

'Well, aren't you the brave heroes? You should have escaped while you had the chance!' sneered Danny Fox as he bared his fearsome teeth at them.

Badger and Gnasher responded by baring their teeth back before they leapt at Danny, each taking off a small chunk of his fur and then speeding away, one to the left and one to the right. It was now a matter of honour and pride for Danny and so, forgetting about the rest, he turned his attentions toward the pursuit of Badger and Gnasher in order to exact his revenge.

While B1 and the others tended to B2, who was only slightly injured, Danny Fox headed off left to pursue Gnasher. Surprised by how fast a creature with such small legs could run, it took him longer than anticipated to catch up with him, although catch up with him he inevitably did. As he was about to pounce and grab Gnasher in his teeth, the lithe cavy suddenly swerved deftly away leaving Danny biting fresh air as Gnasher once again stared into the fox's eyes.

'Come on then—let's get this over with,' demanded Gnasher, with an unreasonable degree of courage.

The two squared up to each other with Gnasher moving dangerously close to those sharp teeth. Just as Gnasher was about to find out how much of a match he was for a creature about ten times his size, Badger, who had been running in from stage right, leapt at Danny's tail. He grabbed it in *his* not inconsiderably sharp teeth, and proceeded to swing round on it like a spider monkey in a tree. Danny, now in pursuit of Badger, found himself quite literally, chasing his own tail.

While all this was happening, the rest of the guinea pigs moved closer, ready to do whatever they could to help out and so Gnasher decided that creating another diversion would be the best course of action. While Danny Fox was spinning in circles, Gnasher was running further away to the left and towards the edge of the field.

Badger decided it was time to let go and the momentum that had been built up from spinning round carried him a few feet away from the dizzy fox. Danny was trying to regain his composure and his sense of direction as Bobby and Co. were snarling at him and so Badger, realising what Gnasher was up to, took the opportunity to run over towards him. As Danny regained his composure, he found himself staring at the faces of the ten creatures who were now confronting him.

'Those two got scared eh—so who's going to save all of you now?' he sneered.

'Hey—Mr Fox—we're over here!' shouted Badger and Gnasher.

'I'll deal with all of you later!' declared Danny as he bounded away in pursuit of his tormentors.

Badger and Gnasher now ran into the long grass at the edge of the field, intent on playing a game of stealth with their foe. When Danny reached the grass he stopped in his tracks, not knowing quite where his prey was. However, his keen nose soon led to the left but just as he was getting dangerously close to Badger, Gnasher popped his head up and shouted over to him from the right-hand side. Although he knew he was close to Badger, he could now see Gnasher and his instinctive reaction was to change course. Yet, when he reached the spot where Gnasher had called out from there was no longer any sight or sound of his cavy foe. While he was trying to get a *fix* on him by employing his sense of smell, Badger called out to him from a little distance away.

Badger had run out of the long grass and into the middle of a path by the side of the next field. Danny sensed his opportunity as Badger no longer had the cover of the grass and was now a *sitting duck*. As Danny quickly closed in on him, Badger was beginning to realise that he may have made a fatal error in leaving his cover and, although he feared the worst, he faced up bravely to his deadly enemy. Badger had resigned himself to the idea that his number was about to be up when Danny Fox suddenly turned tail and ran off in the opposite direction. Badger was thinking that he must look far more fearsome than he had ever imagined. He was soon to discover the real reason behind Danny's change of heart.

He could now hear the sound of barking a little way behind him and a voice shouted, 'go get him boy!' The voice in question was that of Farmer Billing who was out walking his trusty hound Sullivan.

As soon as Sullivan had picked up the scent of fox he was away in pursuit. His master, however, also had Danny in his sights and a shot rang out from his twelve-bore rifle. The pellets whistled over Danny's head but the twin threat from Farmer Billing and Sullivan was enough to convince him that he should abandon any notion of supper and head for a safe haven where he would remain for the many long hours before night fell once again.

As Danny disappeared out of sight, Sullivan was now picking up an altogether different scent and one with which he was quite unfamiliar. Badger, realising now that he might not be safe after all, ran back towards the long grass. Just before Sullivan could reach him Badger spotted a small hole in the ground and ran straight into it.

'What do you think you're doing?—don't you know that you're trespassing?' fumed a creature slightly bigger than himself and with long ears.

'I'm terribly sorry but I'm hiding from a big dog,' Badger explained.

'Oh, I see,' the rabbit replied in an altogether more understanding voice, 'well, mum's the word—we'll keep quiet until he goes away. By the way, my name's Hopkin.'

'Pleased to meet you Hopkin, my name's Bad...,' but Badger was cut short by the terrible whine of Sullivan as he tried to push his snout into the hole.

Fortunately, Sullivan was never going to be able to reach in and they soon heard Farmer Billing shouting to him, 'come away Sullivan, it's only rabbits—come on boy!'

Sullivan reluctantly obeyed his master and abandoned the pursuit. After a short wait Badger decided it was safe to emerge, thanking Hopkin for his help as he went.

'You're welcome Bad, just you take care of yourself now,' replied Hopkin.

Badger found his relieved companions close by and he and Gnasher were congratulated by everyone for their efforts. B1 was also full of admiration for her sister and proud of how bravely she had acted in order to save her life, although B2 made the modest claim, 'anyone would have done it'.

'Have you noticed how Badger and Gnasher haven't argued since we set off?' observed Patrick.

'I think they're just too focused on the mission,' Cedric suggested.

Badger and Gnasher had been talking to each other a few feet away when Gnasher suddenly rounded on his brother.

He angrily enquired, 'what on earth were you playing at running into the middle of the path like that? It was pure luck that that dog came along when it did!'

'I think you spoke too soon,' groaned B1 to Patrick as Badger defended his corner and the argument raged on.

When the altercation eventually fizzled out the companions decided that they should be getting on their way. So, by 7.30am they were heading across their fourth field with only two more to go before they would reach the perimeter of Billings Farm. Progress was steady but slow and the journey across the last two fields passed without event. It was approaching nine o'clock when they eventually reached the side of the road that bordered the farm. The road was busy at that time and they decided that, with weariness setting in, they should rest before tackling the tricky problem of crossing it. They looked across to the opposite side where trees dominated their field of vision.

CHAPTER SEVEN

LOST IN THE WOODS

It was as the group were resting by the roadside that Mrs Fitchett went to open up the outhouse. The scene that greeted her this particular morning filled her with horror and panic. She knew straight away that something was dreadfully amiss when she saw the outhouse door swung open. She ran in fearing the worst and screamed when she saw so many empty hutches with their doors wide open. Mr Fitchett heard her screams and came running out to see what the matter was. He was filled with horror too but tried his best to calm the situation down.

'Now, let's see who's still here and who's missing, then we'll try and work out what's happened.'

It didn't take them long to count the seven that remained.

'You poor darlings!' cried Mrs Fitchett as she cradled Flossy in her arms.

It was tough for the ones who had been left behind as well. They felt lonely, worried about their friends and quite helpless.

'There's twenty-six missing,' announced Mrs Fitchett.

'Twenty-five—don't forget we've got Jessie indoors,' said Mr Fitchett.

Mrs Fitchett noticed how subdued the seven remaining guinea pigs were, even Rosie. They had never been so pleased to see Mrs Fitchett and hoped now that their absent friends would soon be returned home.

Meanwhile, Mr Fitchett took a good look round for any clues as to what might have happened. The back gate had not been forced and he reckoned the intruders must have climbed in over the garden fence. He also noticed that Sniffer's Rock had been dislodged and guessed that one of the interlopers had landed on it when jumping into the garden. Mr Fitchett spotted a piece of wood nearby although he did not stop to wonder what it was doing there.

'Why would anyone want to steal our guinea pigs?' cried Mrs Fitchett.

Mr Fitchett expressed his doubts that a kidnap had occurred. 'I suspect the motive was robbery because my lawnmower and spade have gone. I bet they let the poor little mites escape out of devilment.'

'If that *is* the case then they can't have gone far,' replied Mrs Fitchett.

'It depends on how long they've been gone. Sniffer's Rock has been moved and they may have escaped through the gap in the fence into the fields at the back.'

They immediately searched the fields to see if they could find the errant cavies but they were nowhere to be seen. The Fitchetts decided to call the police to report the break-in and robbery, *and* the missing animals.

The officer who turned up agreed with Mr Fitchett's analysis of the situation.

'If there are twenty-five guinea pigs running round out there then I'm sure somebody will spot them. If we hear anything we'll let you know,' the officer reassured them.

Mrs Fitchett decided to phone Billings Farm to see if there had been any sightings.

It was Farmer Billing who answered. 'Guinea pigs? No, oi ain't seen none o' them—oi seen a fox an' a rabbit though.'

Mrs Fitchett thanked him and asked him to let her know if he did see any guinea pigs.

***

At around 10am—about the time the police officer was visiting Fernbrook Cottage—the companions decided they had rested long enough and should now tackle the tricky task of crossing the road. They moved to the roadside together, keeping low in the grass as the occasional car passed. Bobby suggested that they listen out for the noise of cars and make a run for it when it sounded clear. Finally Bobby gave the order to go and they all set off across the road as fast as they could. As usual, Cedric and Sniffer were at the back and hadn't quite made it to the other side when a car came swiftly around the corner. The driver obviously spotted them as the car slowed right down to allow them to get across.

'That was a close thing!' gasped Cedric.

'Well, we've all made it now so let's push on,' insisted Bobby.

They made their way to the edge of the wood and walked to their right for about thirty yards until they found a path leading in. Entering the woods was like entering another world. Sunlight only got through sporadically where there was an occasional gap in the *roof* of leaves and branches. The air was damp and fusty as a result of the lack of sunlight and the atmosphere was a little eerie. There was bracken and fern and a variety of trees and there were many birds of different types and sizes, though none that posed a threat. They continued along the path passing many narrower ones that led off in different directions.

Eventually they reached a crossroads and, after some discussion, and a little disagreement, they decided to continue straight on. A little way further there was a clearing to their left where a number of trees had been cut down and about fifty yards beyond that the main path appeared to veer off to the right. The problem was that two other paths led in different directions, one to the left and the other almost straight ahead.

'Which way now?' asked Patrick.

'I think we should go straight on!' said B1.

'Shouldn't we just keep to the main path?' opined Cedric.

'How about going left?' suggested Charlie.

'Don't be silly!' scoffed B1 and B2.

'I'm inclined to agree with B1,' said Bobby.

No one else did, however, and by a majority decision they decided to keep on the main path that veered to the right. They were feeling tired and hungry now but were determined to keep going, as there was nothing to eat or drink in the woods. After some time they noticed an opening beyond the trees and could see sunlight.

'Look, we've reached the other end of the woods,' squealed Ted excitedly.

When they reached the opening they found themselves in long grass and nettles. Once through them, a field lay ahead but there was no sign of Whitebridge.

'I think we're back where we started,' moaned Freddy.

'Of course we're not, we're miles from there,' B2 assured him.

'We're not back where we started but we have definitely come out on the wrong side,' groaned Bobby.

They headed straight back into the woods. The path looked somehow different now that they were approaching from the opposite direction. Again, there were many smaller paths leading off and, by general consensus, they decided to take the one that led to their right, which they considered to be in a northerly direction.

Some way ahead Bobby suddenly stopped and declared; 'this doesn't seem right!'

'I agree, I think we're going completely the wrong way,' frowned Patrick.

With all the twists and turns nobody was sure anymore and the general feeling was that Patrick might be right. They about-turned and kept going for what seemed an age until eventually they reached a wider path. They all agreed that taking this path was probably the most sensible course of action and duly followed it until they came to a crossroads.

'Looks a lot like the last crossroads,' grunted B2.

'They're all bound to look similar,' said Badger.

A little way ahead there was a clearing to their left.

'Snff, this looks familiar too,' declared Sniffer.

'I don't believe it!' groaned B1 in consternation, 'we've walked all this way and come in a big circle, this is where we were about two hours ago!'

'We could keep going round in the same circle forever!' sighed Patrick.

'I think we should ask someone the way,' stated B2.

'Like who?' protested Gnasher.

'How about him over there?' suggested B1, pointing to a small grey creature with a bushy tail who was standing a short distance away by the foot of an oak tree.

'Well *I'm* not asking him,' Gnasher assured her.

'Nor me,' insisted Cedric, 'I'm sure we'll find the way if we keep looking.'

'*Oh, what is it with men that they won't ask for directions?*' moaned B1 in frustration. 'Come on B2, we'll ask him ourselves.'

'Hello Mr Squirrel,' B1 began.

'Oh, hello!' replied the squirrel.

'We were wondering if you could tell us the way to Whitebridge,' continued B2.

'Whitebridge eh!—well let me see now, hmm—I think it's that way—or maybe that way, umm—or even that way!' the squirrel dithered, as he pointed first west, then south, then east, 'now where did I bury that acorn?'

'So you're not too sure then!' pronounced B1 with polite understatement.

The squirrel shot a puzzled glance at the guinea pigs. 'You're funny looking rats!—where are your tails?'

'We're not rats!' replied Charlie indignantly.

'We're guinea pigs!' stated Dorie.

'You look very small for pigs,' answered the squirrel.

'So, you've no idea where Whitebridge is then?' B2 asked once again.

'Well it's, umm,' began the squirrel.

'Oh no, not again,' B1 responded.

'I've got it!' proclaimed the squirrel.

'Well I hope it's not catching,' declared Patrick.

At that, the squirrel leapt onto the trunk of a nearby oak tree and scampered up it at startling speed. In no time he had reached the very top and, after a quick look round he shouted down, *'it's that way!'* as he pointed north.

'What's your name?' Dorie enquired of the squirrel, who had arrived swiftly back on terra firma.

'All my friends call me Nutty,' he replied.

'I wonder why?' muttered B1 to B2 with a gentle hint of sarcasm.

They were quite fed up with traipsing through the woods but now at least, they could take comfort in the knowledge that they were going in the right direction. It wasn't too long before they finally came to the edge of the wood and the trees gave way to yet another field. Beyond it they could just make out the rooftops of some houses and they realised that their gaze was now set upon Whitebridge.

They continued on their way through long grass and soon came to a clearing. Just ahead they could see a small round brick structure covered by a gable roof. It had a rope suspended beneath it and a handle at the side. B1 decided to have a bit of fun with Patrick and, pointing to the well, asked him if he knew what it was.

'That—oh, it's a…now let me see, I think I know this one, it's a…a…!' Patrick stuttered as he played for time.

'You don't know do you?' mocked B2.

'Yes I do, it's a...a...!' again Patrick stuttered as he put his paw to his mouth.

'Go on then, what is it?' asked B1.

'It's a...a...w...w...e...ll!' stuttered Patrick, playing for more time.

'Very good!—I really didn't think you'd know that one, did you B2?'

'No I didn't!' replied B2, leaving Patrick wondering what he had said to elicit that response from the twins.

Dorie, Freddy and Ted ran ahead to investigate. They noticed a plaque that bore the words *ROEDEAN WELL* and Dorie decided to find out what was inside. She clambered up the short wall and soon found herself looking down into darkness, unable to tell how deep the well was.

Freddy climbed up behind her and urged, 'be careful Dorie, you're too close to the edge.'

Even as he spoke, Dorie lost her balance and toppled into the abyss.

'Dorie!' cried Freddy in panic as he peered down into the darkness.

'Help me!' yelped Dorie.

He could just about make out her silhouette and realised she was clinging desperately to a rope about two feet down. Realising what had happened, Ted called out to the others to come and help. They all ran towards the well but it was Badger and Gnasher who got there first.

'Hang on Dorie!' shouted Badger.

'I don't think I can for much longer!' Dorie cried desperately.

Charlie and Patrick held on to Gnasher's legs while he, in turn, clung to Badger's. Badger stretched to reach Dorie's paw as he dangled precariously in the darkness.

'Just a bit further!' he urged.

This action necessitated Bobby and Cedric hanging on to Charlie and Patrick's legs as well and Badger could now almost reach Dorie's paw. He stretched that little bit more and Gnasher had to clasp his legs even tighter in order not to let go of him.

'Put your paw in mine Dorie!' coaxed Badger.

She did so but was reluctant to let go of the rope with her other paw.

'You must let go now Dorie, trust me I've got you,' Badger assured her.

She was scared to let go but realised the danger she was putting her rescuers in and reluctantly did so. They all pulled each other up and soon Dorie was safe but shaken once again after this, her second personal ordeal.

'Rosie and the other girls were right—there are many dangers in the world!' uttered Freddy, who was also shaken by this latest episode.

'Yes there are, and no one must run off again!' Bobby reprimanded sternly.

After a brief rest they continued across the last field of long grass with the rooftops of Whitebridge remaining in view.

'It's not been so bad getting this far,' stated Patrick.

'You are joking!' B1 frowned, recalling the sparrowhawk incident, the escapade with Danny Fox, getting lost in the woods and this latest ordeal at the well, not to mention the hours of walking their little legs had done.

'Yes, I suppose so,' Patrick agreed, 'I just can't believe we're nearly in Whitebridge.'

Meanwhile, Mr and Mrs Fitchett had arrived at the roadside where the guinea pigs had been seen a couple of hours before. The police had informed the Fitchetts about this after the sighting had been reported by the car driver. They proceeded to scour the surrounding area before eventually abandoning the search. As they looked out across the adjacent field, they could not have known that twelve of their pets, hidden in the long grass, were crossing at that very moment.

It was now a little after 11am and, as the Fitchetts were returning home, the guinea pigs had begun to make their way across the road bridge over the River White that allowed access to the town from the south. On reaching the other side, they took cover under some bushes and surveyed the sprawling urban jungle that lay before them. They realised there was quite a way to go yet before they would have Fanshaw Cosmetics in their sights.

— CHAPTER EIGHT —

WHITEBRIDGE

Before setting off there was a brief discussion about the importance of staying together and of avoiding being spotted by people, dogs or anything else. The plan was simple—if they walked in a straight line they should come out of Whitebridge on the opposite side.

They made their way past many stone-built houses, walking on grass verges when there was one and, once or twice, hiding underneath parked cars to avoid being seen. There were one or two close calls, especially when a tabby cat saw them and began hissing as it peered under the car they were hiding beneath. Badger and Gnasher could do nothing to frighten this stubborn moggie away and it only eventually left them alone when a dog being walked by its owner on the other side of the road, diverted its attention.

Carefully and warily they continued, uphill most of the time it seemed, until they came to a fence of vertical metal bars. There was a grass embankment running steeply down and then up again on the other side, which was enclosed by another metal fence. Between the embankments were four lines of shiny metal that seemed to run forever in both directions.

'What is it?' asked Patrick.

'It's a railway line,' answered Ted.

'Yes, trains run along here,' added B2.

Deciding on a direct route across the line, they squeezed between the metal bars and clambered gingerly down the embankment. Getting across the rails proved a little trickier as the smooth surface was slippery and difficult to grip. There were two sets of tracks and thereby four rails to climb over. Gnasher leapt over first and they pushed and pulled each other over each rail with Badger taking up the rear.

Most of them had made it over the final rail when they heard a sound that was getting progressively louder.

'We must hurry—there's a train coming!' warned B1.

Ted, Dorie and Freddy had been larking about and, along with Badger who was waiting for them, were still between the last two rails. There was now a sense of urgency as Badger hurriedly pushed Ted and Dorie over last rail to safety. Freddy, meanwhile, had tried to climb over but had slipped backwards and was struggling to get up again. Badger went to help him up but the train was looming up fast.

'Come on you two, hurry!' shouted their pals, but the pair couldn't move quickly enough.

When Badger looked up the train was only yards away.

'They won't make it!' screamed B1.

Badger, realising there was no time for them to get off, pounced on Freddy, holding him down between the rails as the train passed overhead.

The ten watching guinea pigs looked on in horror and were too shocked to speak. The train seemed to take an age to pass but when it did they could see Badger lying down flat with Freddy underneath him. Dorie cried out in panic and all of them feared the worst as Badger and Freddy lay still. Gnasher ran over first and shook Badger but he didn't move.

'Oh no!' exclaimed Gnasher.

Just then, Badger tilted his head sideways before getting up and pulling Freddy to his feet. They were all tremendously relieved and Badger thanked Gnasher for showing such concern.

'It was the youngster that I was worried about,' Gnasher assured him.

The three clambered over the last rail and all of them now made their way up the far embankment, through the fence and into the street. They crossed a road and then walked along the next street before coming to a parade of shops at the other end. This part of Whitebridge was quite busy so they had to be extra vigilant. On the corner was a shop that sold newspapers and confectionary and other things besides.

'Look at all those cigarettes!' whooped Cedric as he noticed the various brands on the wall behind the shopkeeper.

'Trust you Cedric!' barked B2.

'Look at all those lettuces!' noted Patrick as he surveyed the greengrocers next door to the newsagents.

The lettuces, as well as many other items of fruit and vegetables, were on display at the front of the shop and were a very inviting sight to the hungry guinea pigs.

'Look at all those cucumbers!' beamed Freddy.

'Look at all those tomatoes!' Dorie drooled.

'Snff, look at all those carrots!' snorted Sniffer as Charlie nodded in agreement.

'We can get a good lunch here and it will set us up for the rest of the day,' Badger enthused.

'We can't just walk up and help ourselves—we'll be spotted straight away,' argued B1.

'She's absolutely right,' Patrick agreed.

'Maybe there'll be some scraps to eat at the back of the shop,' suggested Bobby.

They carefully made their way round by the back of the newsagents and along to the next gate. Bobby squeezed beneath it and entered cautiously before giving the all-clear to the others. They found crates that were mainly empty but had a few scraps in them, including lettuce and cabbage leaves as well as half a cucumber. There were also some apples that were beginning to go bad but were largely edible and there were, as Sniffer was the first to discover, a couple of carrots.

They all gratefully tucked into this unexpected feast but were startled when the back door of the shop opened suddenly. It was the owner bringing another empty crate outside. However, he hesitated for a moment as he surveyed the yard but the cavies had moved stealthily out of sight.

'What's wrong dear?' a woman's voice called out.

'I'm not sure—I think it might be rats again,' the man replied.

'We must get that yard cleaned up!' declared the woman.

The door closed and the cavies emerged from their hiding places, once again tucking into whatever they could find. Freddy and Dorie were chewing a piece of cucumber when they were suddenly confronted by two creatures of a similar size to themselves.

'What do you think you're doing?—this is our patch!' protested one.

'Yeah, now clear off or else!' said the other.

'Or else what?' asked Freddy.

'Or else we'll...,' but the creature stopped in his tracks when he realised he and his mate were outnumbered.

Charlie and Patrick came over to sort the problem out.

'Listen up rats, we gotta eat!' said Charlie abrasively.

'Yeah, so why don't you push off!' cut in Patrick.

'Why should we?' came the reply.

Because there are twelve of us!' announced Patrick.

'There might be twelve of you but just wait till we tell our big brothers!' blurted the rat as he and his mate backed away.

'Oh, I'm so scared!' Patrick mocked as the rats ran off down the road. 'Ha, big brothers—I don't think so,' he laughed.

'Anyway, I do think we should eat up and be on our way,' said Bobby, who was beginning to feel that they had lingered long enough.

They carefully made their way out of the yard and back to the shop fronts when they all suddenly dived for cover. It was sheer luck that they avoided being spotted by Mr and Mrs Fitchett as the couple climbed out of their car and walked towards the shops. They knew they had to stay out of sight although Sniffer and Cedric had a secret yearning to be caught right there and then. The Fitchetts soon emerged and climbed back into their car. As they were driving off, Patrick saw the newsagent put one of the pieces of paper in his shop window and walked up close enough to see. It read;

MISSING, 25 GUINEA PIGS, REWARD FOR THEIR SAFE RETURN

When Patrick told the others what it said, they all agreed that they needed to get out of Whitebridge sooner rather than later.

'What's that in the distance?' asked Ted as he looked up the hill to the side of the shops.

'Aren't they those rats?' said B1.

'Snff, I think they are?' agreed Sniffer.

'Only this time there's a few more of them and the others seem a bit bigger,' observed Cedric.

'Right—well anyway, I do think we should get going now,' urged Bobby, and soon they were all heading swiftly down the road.

***

It was approaching 2.00pm when, over at Fanshaw Cosmetics, Cuthbert Fanshaw was about to inspect the new incumbents at his laboratory. He had been busy at a meeting all morning and was now quite excited about seeing the guinea pigs that Brian and Bill had brought him from Crickley Meadow.

His excitement was certainly not about to be shared by the captured cavies. When they arrived they had been thrown into three hutches between them. Pauline and her girls were in one hutch while Sandy, Smokey, Cyril and Dylan were in another. Boo, Joey, Emily, Cleo and Flossy were in the third hutch, which, like the others, was pretty, much devoid of home comforts. There was a little bit of sawdust but no hay and the water bottles were empty. At first they were all too stunned to bother about anything but now they were feeling very fed up. Monica was bemoaning the lack of a mirror and Smokey was most upset.

'I do hope we can go home soon,' she groaned to Sandy.

She missed the Fitchetts and right now all she wanted to do was run around the garden at Fernbrook Cottage. The worst thing for all of them was that they didn't know what was happening or if they were ever going to see home or all their other friends again. It was a very unhappy group that Cuthbert Fanshaw beheld that afternoon.

'Excellent work you two!' Cuthbert beamed to Brian and Bill, 'these will do nicely. They're a miserable lot but they're going to be a lot more miserable when we start on them, ha, ha, ha!'

'When's that going to be?' asked Bill.

'Tomorrow—we'll have fifteen by then as we've got two more coming in today. I've very kindly offered them a good home,' laughed Cuthbert.

Three laboratory workers came in at that point.

'Here you are—what do you think?' asked Cuthbert.

They all agreed that these were fine specimens and they were very much looking forward to beginning the experiments.

All this talk of experiments, plus being surrounded by unsavoury looking characters, was making the guinea pigs feel decidedly uncomfortable.

'I like the look of this one—such beautiful fur!' bleated one of the laboratory workers as he pointed to Monica. 'It almost seems a shame that I've got to shave a big patch of it off tomorrow so that I can put some chemicals on her bare skin!' he continued in a sinister tone.

'I do hope someone will come to rescue us,' cried Maisie, when the men had left the room.

'But who?—if the Fitchetts knew we were here they would have come by now surely?' moaned Monica.

'Maybe Bobby or Badger and Gnasher will come for us,' Tufty speculated, more out of hope than anything else.

'It's a nice thought but how likely is that?' groaned Pauline.

I hope something happens thought Smokey as she contemplated the stark reality of the situation.

They would certainly have taken comfort had they known that twelve of their friends were trundling through Whitebridge at that very moment with rescue in mind.

***

Good progress was made through the town and they had been clever enough, or fortunate enough, to evade capture up to now. They regularly had to hide from people and they were forced to take cover once again as a young girl and her mother came out of a building that had a sign above the door bearing the legend;

SCHOOL OF SONG AND DANCE

The girl was carrying a violin case and as she came closer Charlie was suddenly consumed by a desperate panic as he implored everyone to keep their heads down.

'Ok, keep calm!' insisted Cedric.

'We've got to be careful Charlie, admittedly, but there's really no need to panic,' Bobby assured him.

'*Oh, but there is!*' Charlie protested.

'Come on now, she's only a young girl to be sure—hardly dangerous,' asserted Patrick.

'But that's *exactly* what she is!' squealed Charlie.

'What on earth do you mean?' asked Bobby in bemusement.

'Don't you see—*she's got a gun!*'

B1 ended the confusion. 'Don't be ridiculous Charlie, that's not a gun, it's a violin!'

'Well it looks like a gun to me!'

This episode was the source of some amusement as Charlie and his companions took cover until the coast was clear. Shortly after resuming their journey they found themselves climbing through railings once again, this time entering a public park. It was a large park with paths that criss-crossed beds of flowers and shrubs and circled a lake. Beyond the lake was an area of well-kept grass where children were playing. They decided it was safest to move amongst the shrubs and flowerbeds. As they got closer to the lake they suddenly heard a strange *whirring* noise and stopped in their tracks, wondering where on earth it was coming from.

Sniffer was first to notice a small car that had stopped on the path close by and curiosity got the better of him. He could not resist the temptation to investigate more closely even though Bobby and Patrick were urging him to come back. Freddy was also curious and he thought that if it was ok for Sniffer to check it out then it was ok for him as well.

When Freddy reached the open-topped car, Sniffer had already climbed onto the seat.

'Hey Sniffer, this is cool!' Freddy cried out excitedly.

'Snff, I wonder how it got here?' replied Sniffer.

Freddy decided to climb on board as well.

'I've never been in a car like this before—do you think it was made especially for guinea pigs?' asked Freddy.

'I don't know,' Sniffer answered as he placed his front paws on the steering wheel.

The others were screaming at them to come back when all of a sudden the whirring noise started up again.

'Snff, I think we should get out now,' suggested Sniffer, although Freddy protested.

Before they could do anything the car lurched forward very suddenly and they were thrown back into their seats with Sniffer clutching the steering wheel for dear life. Very soon they were hurtling along the path at breakneck speed. Freddy found it thrilling but poor Sniffer was terrified, especially when the car lurched round a corner virtually on two wheels. It continued to zigzag along the meandering paths and even did a circuit of the lake.

'Hey Sniffer, this is great fun isn't it?' whooped Freddy, but Sniffer only whined and winced back.

All the time the watching guinea pigs looked on in astonishment as they saw their pals riding round at great speed.

'I never knew Sniffer could drive like that!' declared Patrick.

'Who does he think he is—Lewis Hamilton?' B1 asked rhetorically.

'He's certainly surprised me,' frowned Bobby as he peered across to the other side of the lake where a small boy was watching the car's every move.

He was holding a small metal box with an antenna and he seemed very amused as he watched the car race along. Freddy was getting more and more excited but Sniffer was feeling more and more ill.

'I'm loving this!' declared Freddy.

'I do wish it would stop!' groaned Sniffer.

As if on cue, the car veered off the path in the direction of the lake and came to a sudden halt. The jolt sent Sniffer hurtling over the top of the car before tumbling down into the lake. Freddy had managed to hold on more tightly and had remained in the car but he now climbed out to go and look for Sniffer.

'Nice wheels!' purred Freddy in admiration, looking back as he went.

Meanwhile, the boy turned excitedly to his mother sitting on a bench close by.

'Did you see that mum?' he cried, 'there were two small animals riding round in my car!'

His mother looked over but there was no sign of any animals.

'Oh Johnny, you've got such a vivid imagination!'

Johnny's protests fell on deaf ears as his mother told him it was time to go home.

The whirring noise started once more and the car drove off, this time devoid of passengers. Freddy climbed down to the edge of the lake but when he realised that Sniffer was nowhere to be seen he panicked and cried out for help.

They all dashed over to the lakeside and Patrick was just about to dive in when Sniffer emerged looking like a drowned rat. He stood on the bank and shook off the excess water before looking up to see eleven pairs of eyes staring at him.

'Thank goodness you're alright!' stammered Patrick.

'You should thank your lucky stars you are!' fumed Bobby. What on earth were you playing at? You could have got us all caught or worse still, injured or drowned yourself or young Freddy here!'

'Really Sniffer, you should know better than to go joyriding at your age!' Cedric remonstrated.

'Yes, snff, I'm sorry, it won't happen again,' Sniffer assured him.

'Let's hope it doesn't,' Bobby grunted before instructing them all to get moving again.

Once out of the park they were looking across an estate that sloped gently downhill. Beyond it they could see green fields and it was apparent to them that they should soon be leaving Whitebridge behind.

'Come on—just one more estate,' urged Bobby.

Cedric and Sniffer were, as usual, at the back but Sniffer found that he had to slow down to allow Cedric to catch up with him.

'I'm sorry Sniffer, I'm feeling breathless—oh for a ciggie!' moaned Cedric.

'If you ask me it's all those cigarettes that have made you like this and, snff, to tell you the truth, I think you're better off without them!' Sniffer asserted bluntly.

'Now that's a little harsh,' objected Cedric, taken aback by Sniffer's uncharacteristic directness.

'Maybe, but I'm going to catch up with the others so you'd better move a bit quicker!'

As Sniffer caught up, Charlie and Patrick looked back and called out to Cedric to hurry up. Cedric protested that he was coming as fast as he could but just then they all became aware of a person moving rather quickly along the pavement.

'He's walking fast!' shouted Freddy.

'Only he's not walking—he's on wheels!' noted Ted.

They all ran for whatever cover they could find, apart from Cedric who could hardly move at all by now. Unfortunately, the boy spotted him and jumped off his skateboard. Although Cedric was scared he was unable to move and when the boy approached him he remained *frozen* to the spot and was easily caught.

'Well, what have we got here then?' beamed the youth gleefully as he held Cedric aloft with one hand as if he were a trophy. 'I'm going to have some fun with you—you're going to regret that you ever fell into the hands of *Kurt Sting*!'

'*Kurt Sting!*' the younger guinea pigs all hissed as they fell over each other whilst furtively stepping backwards. They all looked helplessly on and Sniffer was feeling extremely guilty for leaving Cedric behind. Kurt Sting carried his *prey* a short distance, placed his skateboard on the ground and put Cedric on top of a wall.

'Now I want you to keep still!' protested Kurt Sting as Cedric kept wriggling. 'Ok, have it your way, I'll just have to tie you up then—we can't have you moving around when I'm trying to aim at you, can we?'

The youth felt in his pocket for a piece of string while everyone looked on in horror as their terrified companion had his paws bound.

'We've got to do something,' spluttered Badger and Gnasher.

'But what can we do?' asked Patrick.

'I've got an idea,' said B1 as she whispered to the others.

'Right, let's give it a try,' agreed Bobby.

As Kurt Sting was busily tying a knot, the group crept across the road. While the rest hid behind the kerb, B1 and B2 walked towards Kurt Sting's training shoes as Badger and Gnasher moved towards the skateboard that was on the ground nearby.

B1 and B2 set quickly to work. First they untied the youth's shoelaces before tying a lace from each shoe together, just as they had tied the pieces of string in the garden the previous day.

'There—done!' whispered B1 as the twins moved to join the others behind the kerb.

'I don't think you'll be going anywhere,' grunted Kurt Sting to Cedric, who was tightly bound. 'All I need now is a few nice rocks.'

As he turned away from the wall he lost his footing and fell over backwards.

'What the...?' he cried but even as he was falling, Badger and Gnasher were manoeuvring the skateboard with their teeth. As Kurt Sting landed squarely on top, the brothers guided it along the pavement while the youth's arms and legs were flailing helplessly about. They kept the skateboard in their teeth until they reached the brow of a hill that sloped sharply away and then, with one last shove, released it and watched as it flew over the kerb and down the road out of control.

All the guinea pigs, apart from poor Cedric, came to watch as the skateboard eventually careered into a kerb on the other side where the road bent to the right. The hapless Kurt Sting went flying into the air and landed in a tree in the front garden of a house while his skateboard flew still further, smashing through the lounge window. A very angry man came out shaking his fists.

'Kurt Sting—I might have known you'd have something to do with this—just wait till I speak to your father—*and you'll be paying for this window!*' he screeched.

The guinea pigs were extremely amused by what they had just witnessed and very pleased with themselves but now they realised they had to rescue Cedric from his lofty perch.

'Do you think you can jump?' Patrick asked rather stupidly.

Even if Cedric's paws weren't bound together there's no way he could survive a fall from that height.

'What about the Cavy tower?' suggested Dorie.

'Brilliant idea!' beamed Bobby as a few hearts sank at the prospect of doing that all over again.

Still, they realised it had to be done and proceeded to faithfully reconstruct the tower just as it had been at Fernbrook Cottage that same morning, although that now seemed a very long time ago.

It was B1 who scaled the tower and was just able to reach up and climb on to the top of the wall where she then nibbled through the string to free Cedric's paws. Cedric was a little sheepish about clambering down but was being urged on, particularly by those at the bottom. B1 encouraged him to descend backwards and not look down. This he did and, to the relief of everyone, he was soon on the ground along with B1, after which the tower dismantled itself.

As they all set off on their way past the last estate they noticed a police car parked outside the house where Kurt Sting had landed and watched him being put inside.

The group were now very keen to leave Whitebridge and it was not long before they had reached the edge of the estate and were looking out across the fields that bordered it.

'Snff, do you think we're going in the right direction?' asked Sniffer.

'I'm not sure but my guess is that we should head for that wooded area over there beyond the fields,' replied Bobby.

'Not another wood!' moaned Patrick.

'How about a rest?' enquired Cedric.

'Yes, I think we all need one, but let's get further away from Whitebridge first,' suggested Bobby.

They all stopped halfway across that first field and basked in the early evening sunshine, letting the cares of the day wash over them as they prepared themselves for the long evening ahead. They must have rested for over an hour and there was only sporadic conversation. Dorie had been lying close to Sniffer and had looked in deep thought for a short while.

'Why do they call you Sniffer?' she suddenly asked.

Sniffer contemplated the question. 'Snff...dunno!' he replied after a few seconds.

'Oh!' whispered Dorie.

Badger and Gnasher were starting to get restless and suggested they should get on their way. Although Cedric and Sniffer would happily have rested longer, there was no real protest when it was decided to continue on the journey in the direction of the woods. It appeared to be a much smaller wooded area than the previous one and Bobby was confident they could navigate their way through it. Even so, they were worried about the possibility of getting lost again and decided it would be best to ask the way if they got the chance.

A few minutes after entering the woods, Ted noticed a creature standing about ten yards away.

'Isn't that Nutty?' he asked.

'It can't be—Nutty's from the *other* side of Whitebridge,' B2 replied.

'And he's a different colour—Nutty was grey but this one's red,' added B1.

As they approached the squirrel he looked up and proclaimed, 'well bless my soul, you're very odd looking rabbits!'

'We're not rabbits, we're guinea pigs!' explained Patrick.

'We were wondering if you could help us—we're trying to get to Fanshaw Cosmetics,' said Bobby.

'Oh, well now, let me see,' the squirrel replied.

'You could always climb up a tree like your mate Nutty did,' suggested Dorie.

'Nutty?—oh yes, I know of him—he's not the type I'd call a mate.' Then he added in a whispered tone as if worried that unseen ears might hear, *'he's a grey squirrel—very common you know!* Anyhow, there'll be no need for climbing up trees—if you keep going in this direction you'll get to where you're going,' he told them as he pointed northwards.

'What's your name?' asked Dorie.

'Rupert—at your service,' the squirrel replied, bowing as he spoke.

They thanked him and soon made their way beyond the trees. Sheep were grazing on the lush grass of the field that lay before them and downhill in the distance a group of large buildings were now clearly visible.

That's got to be Fanshaw's place thought Bobby.

They looked across to where the sun reflected off the building's aluminium roof, framed by the green of the Penfold Hills rolling gently into the distance.

The last part of the journey passed without event and the sheep didn't even seem to notice the unusual visitors that snaked their way through the grass. In less than an hour they had crossed three fields, keeping a safe distance from a farmhouse, before they eventually came to the main road. They took care crossing it and found themselves standing at the foot of a tall perimeter fence that surrounded a cluster of buildings. Close by a sign read;

FANSHAW COSMETICS LIMITED

'Well done everybody, we've made it!' declared Bobby.

'Now all we've got to do is to get in without being seen, rescue our friends, get out and then find our way back home!' stated Patrick wryly.

CHAPTER NINE

THE RAID

The group sneaked along the perimeter fence towards the gate. They clambered beneath and entered the yard. They were now about twenty yards from the main entrance and Badger moved forward slightly to peer in through the glass doors.

'Is there anyone in there?' asked Charlie.

'Yes, there's a man wearing a peaked cap, sitting down at a desk but he seems to be asleep,' replied Badger.

'He must have been out in the garden all day!' reasoned Dorie.

'He'll be the night time security guard,' stated Cedric, who knew about these things from his time in a laboratory.

'Well, he's not watching much if he's asleep!' observed Patrick.

'No, and that's lucky for us!' said Bobby.

They felt sure that there was no one else around apart from the sleeping man in the foyer. The car park was empty and it was now quite late in the evening. It was time to go in!

Charlie suggested they should split up into groups of two or three so that each group could approach from different sides of the building. The suggestion caused some unease and the general consensus was that they should stick together.

'We have to split up—it's the proper way to do it—I saw it in a movie!' insisted Charlie.

After a short discussion it was reluctantly decided upon that they would indeed split up into groups as Charlie suggested. There would be B1, B2 and Ted forming one group while Bobby, Freddy and Dorie would make up another trio. Badger and Gnasher, Charlie and Patrick, and Cedric and Sniffer made up three more pairs.

Bobby gave the order. 'Let's go—be careful everyone!'

They now began to circumnavigate the building, B1 and Bobby's groups going off to the left, Badger and Gnasher to the middle and Charlie and Cedric's groups to the right. Bobby ushered Freddy and Dorie to the rear of the building wishing B1, B2 and Ted luck as he left them at the side.

The latter group were now left to their own devices and Ted suddenly felt quite important. This is where the real adventure begins, he thought. He had seen plenty of adventures on the telly but he never expected to find himself in a real-life one. Now he had the opportunity to be a hero if only he could find a way in to rescue his kidnapped friends.

He soon spotted a metal staircase that led down below ground level and suggested that the three should climb down to see what was at the bottom. They all agreed and they gingerly descended, leaping one step at a time until they found themselves on a concrete floor. They were standing in front of a red painted metal door. They tried to push it but it was no good.

'I can't see a way in here,' groaned B2.

'Looking for a way in are you?—perhaps we can be of assistance!'

The startled trio spiralled round to see five rats quickly emerging through a gap that they'd failed to spot moments before. They thought about making a run for it but realised it was hopeless. There was no choice but to surrender and they were soon prodded through the gap and marched off into the building. The three were devastated at being caught but Ted felt worst of all. It had been his suggestion to go down the stairs in the first place and now the adventure was over and, along with it, the chance of glory.

Meanwhile, Charlie and Patrick parted company with Cedric and Sniffer who carried on towards the side of the building.

Cedric walked on keeping slightly ahead.

'Well Sniffer, I think we should be really proud of what we've achieved today, I'll bet there are not many guinea pigs that have ever walked that far or had the kind of adventures we've had. Don't you feel proud Sniffer?' There was no reply. 'Sniffer, *Sniffer?*' Cedric called out as he looked round but he could not even see his friend now.

He walked back a little way to where he thought Sniffer should have been but all he found was a manhole cover that was partially open. Cedric peered in through the gap and called out to Sniffer once again but as he waited for an answer, he suddenly realised that he was surrounded by three rats.

'Gottcha!' one rasped as they grabbed Cedric and dragged him away. 'Now you can go and join the rest of your friends!'

Cedric desperately hoped that they were referring to the friends that were taken from the outhouse and not his fellow pursuers.

They manhandled Cedric towards the main building and squeezed him through a small hole that the rats used regularly to come and go. He was marched for some considerable distance until they eventually started to climb some stairs. This was hard work for Cedric as the stairs were designed for people and not guinea pigs and each step required a huge effort.

'You might lose some of that weight with all this exercise!' one rat teased.

Before long they had reached the top and Cedric was then led along a corridor.

'This is where you'll be going, I'm sure you'll love it here!' hissed one of his captors sarcastically.

He pointed to a room that had a door with frosted glass at the top. The door was locked but the rats, of course, knew another way in. Cedric was led through an air vent and when he emerged on the other side he realised that this was the very room that he and his companions had set off to find. However, he had not intended to find it in this manner.

'Dad, is that you!' called out Sandy from a cage over towards the window.

'Yes, it is,' replied Cedric.

'Shut up!' cried a rat as he took Cedric to one of the cages. He was made to climb up with the help of a chair and the rat then used a stick to open the cage before forcing Cedric to climb in.

'Now you lot behave yourselves while we go looking for the rest of you creatures.'

'There aren't any more, I've come here alone!' lied Cedric unconvincingly.

Just then, B1, B2 and Ted were marched into the room and Cedric's heart sank.

'Come alone have you?' sneered the rat to Cedric. 'Right men, let's lock them up, then we'll go and see if we can find any more of these tailless wonders!'

As soon as the rats had gone Cedric shouted across the room and established that all thirteen of the original captives were present.

Then he proceeded to explain how he had come to be there and told them about his experiences on the journey from Crickley Meadow.

'Oh, Cedric, you *are* a hero!' purred Maisie after listening to Cedric's stories.

'Do you know what they plan to do with us here?' asked Cedric.

'Experiments!' announced a voice from the back of Cedric's cage.

'Who are you?' Cedric asked, looking round to where the voice was coming from.

'My name's Eric,' replied a buff and white Abyssinian male guinea pig.

'And I'm Bruno,' added another shorthaired brown and white guinea pig.

'Bruno?—don't I know you from somewhere?' Cedric asked.

'You know, I think I remember you as well—weren't you at that laboratory where they put us on smoking duty?' recalled Bruno.

'Yes, of course!' remembered Cedric. 'You don't happen to have a ciggie do you?' he asked hopefully.

'No, I gave them up as soon as I was rescued—it's a mugs game if you ask me!' Bruno replied.

'Didn't you find it difficult?' asked Cedric.

'No,' said Bruno, 'just a bit of will power and it was easy, and I must say I feel a lot better for it!'

'I don't suppose there's any chance of us being on smoking duty here then?' moaned Cedric, searching for consolation in his current predicament.

'We're not going to be on any kind of duty!' Eric protested. 'You haven't come all this way just to give up now have you?'

'No, of course not!' replied Cedric, suddenly remembering his mission, although he did feel a little helpless locked up in a cage.

While the rats had been capturing Cedric, Sniffer was wondering how he had come to be in this dark, wet and smelly place. He had of course, fallen into the open manhole and landed in an underground sewer. The only light he could see was coming from the opening he had fallen through but it was too far up for him to contemplate climbing back out. He decided to start crawling along the sewer to search for another means of escape.

As he crawled he occasionally slipped down into slimy liquid and was soon covered in the unpleasant substance. His sight was just beginning to adjust to the darkness when he thought he could see something moving a short distance ahead. Once again he slipped down into the liquid and, upon making a splash, Sniffer was startled to hear a voice call out to him.

'Oi, you!—keep up with the rest of us!'

It now dawned on Sniffer that he had stumbled upon a company of rats who were patrolling the sewer. It appeared they had mistaken him for one of their own—not difficult in the poor light, especially given Sniffer's long rat-like nose and the fact that he was covered in sewage. His first instinct was to turn and run but he thought better of it and decided that his best option was to walk behind the rats, though keeping a safe enough distance to avoid blowing his cover. He was careful not to turn his back on them for fear they would notice that there was something different about him.

'I thought I told you to keep up!' the rat called out to Sniffer once again.

'Yeah, come on, keep up with me, do you think I smell or something?' grunted the rat closest to Sniffer.

'Snff...n...no,' Sniffer mumbled as he dared to move a little closer.

He made up his mind that he was going to try and escape as soon as a half chance presented itself. The smell was almost unbearable for poor old Sniffer although it didn't seem to bother the rats. He was beginning to wonder how much more of this he could take and was sure the rat at the back was going to get wise to him very soon. All of a sudden, as he squinted in the darkness, he thought he could make out what appeared to be an inlet in the wall. Sniffer knew that this could be his chance. He approached the inlet nervously, keeping as close behind the last rat as he dared. Upon reaching the inlet, he stopped for a couple of seconds while summoning up the courage to make a dive for it.

He was still contemplating it when a rat called out again.

'*Hey you!*—how many times do I have to tell you?—*stop lagging behind!*'

Sniffer was now facing the wall and the rat at the back noticed something strange.

'He hasn't got a tail!' he declared.

'*Hasn't got a tail?* bawled another, 'he can't be one of us then—*grab him!*'

Sniffer now had no choice. He made a dive for the opening in the wall and, as he did so, the closest rat lurched forward to try and ensnare him but ended up face down in the sewer.

'Drat! I went to grab him by his tail but he hasn't got one,' growled the disgruntled creature.

'Fool!—get after him all of you!' screamed the leader.

Sniffer was now running through a narrow tunnel that twisted and turned and spiralled uphill. Being acutely aware that his pursuers were close behind, Sniffer was running faster than he had ever done in his life. He was beginning to get out of breath but didn't dare slow down. He was thinking that a pair of grubby paws might grab him at any moment when suddenly, a shaft of light appeared a short distance away. It's source was a pipe that fed into the tunnel and Sniffer crawled along it towards the light. Upon squeezing through the gap at the end of the pipe, Sniffer found himself standing on shiny white porcelain but when he peered over the edge, he realised that he was a little way off the ground.

After a quick look round it became apparent that jumping was the only means of escape. As Sniffer stood on the edge he was very hesitant until the head of a rat appeared through the hole. With no time for further deliberation, he leapt to the ground. It seems Sniffer must have been more lithe and athletic than he had realised as the landing did not cause him any injury at all. A door on the other side of the room was slightly ajar and he was just able to squeeze through the narrow opening.

Sniffer found himself in a very large room full of boxes and machinery and, to his right, a metal staircase. Realising the rats would not be far behind, he made a decision. A rat appeared just as Sniffer was jumping onto the first step. There were nine steps in all and, with each one, Sniffer half expected to be pulled back from behind and led away to an unknown fate. With a huge effort he managed to reach the top and found himself standing on a raised platform. On glancing down and seeing the three rats in hot pursuit, Sniffer turned to run.

One side of the platform was blocked off by a large pair of tightly shut metal doors and the other side was too high up to contemplate jumping. Sniffer realised he was cornered.

'Gotcha now!' proclaimed a rat, 'we'll soon have you in that laboratory over there with your friends.'

Sniffer looked round to see a door on a mezzanine floor across the warehouse. He had discovered the location of the room he was searching for but the information seemed of little use to him now. As he was glancing round he noticed a hook hanging down on the end of a chain. This, in turn, was looped over a strong wire by a pulley that allowed the hook to travel between the platform and the warehouse below. The hook was, in fact, used to transport boxes from the warehouse to the platform, ready for despatch.

Sniffer was now desperate and, just as the rats were closing in, he lunged towards the hook and clung on to it for dear life. It was an instinctive action and, he believed, probably a futile one. The first rat reached out to grab Sniffer as he hung with his feet dangling in thin air. Sensing their prey was at last within their grasp, the rats were astonished when the hook, chain *and* Sniffer suddenly began to slide away in the direction of the warehouse below. Sniffer's weight and momentum had been enough to set the chain in motion.

'Drat that creature having no tail!' groaned a rat in exasperation.

'Come on, we can't let him get away, how would we explain it to the sarg?' yelled another as they turned and ran back down the stairs.

As he slid away down the wire, Sniffer desperately clung on as the momentum rapidly increased.

Just as Sniffer had been trying to escape the clutches of the rats, Charlie and Patrick had been making their way into the building. They had walked down a short corridor and found themselves in the same warehouse that Sniffer had arrived in via the sewer. Feeling quite pleased with themselves, they were looking for a way through past the boxes and crates when they found their passage blocked by two large rodents.

'Where do you think you're going?' enquired one of them.

'To rescue our friends,' replied Charlie.

'Did you hear that Reg? We've got a couple of brave ones here!'

'Brave, but stupid!' snarled Reg.

'We've come a long way to get here and if you think we're going to let a couple of squirts like you stop us now, you'd better think again!' bellowed Charlie with a brazenness that astounded Patrick.

'Yes…th-think again!' stammered Patrick, trying to sound convincing.

'Poo, what's that smell?' sneered Charlie, grimacing as he held his nose.

'Are you sayin' it's us wot smell?' Reg challenged him.

'Yes I am—*you dirty rat!*' hissed Charlie as he did his utmost to wind the creatures up, much to Patrick's increasing discomfiture.

'Well let's see what you're made of then,' fired back the other rat.

'Right then!' cried Charlie bravely as he raised his clenched paws.

Patrick was standing just behind Charlie as the creatures moved towards them. When they got within striking distance Charlie raised his right paw. Patrick could not bear to look and closed his eyes. As Charlie hit out with his paw he shut his eyes also.

At that very moment Sniffer was careering along the wire, having built up quite a speed. He was relieved to have escaped the clutches of the rats but was now gripped by a new fear. What would happen when the hook reached the end of the wire and how would he get down? As he was contemplating this, Sniffer realised that he was struggling to maintain his grip on the hook. Desperate as he was, Sniffer was unable to cling on and, upon letting go, he glanced down and saw the warehouse floor looming towards him at great speed. Sniffer shut his eyes, hoping for the best but fearing the worst. Bracing himself for the impact, he felt his rear end bang into something soft. He bounced off in a different direction and, this time landed with a splash in half a bucket of water.

The rat did not know what had hit him as Sniffer's impact caused him to crash into the head of his mate. As the second rat fell, his head hit Charlie's outstretched paw before the hapless rodents dropped to the floor unconscious. If Charlie was slightly surprised by the scene that greeted him when he opened his eyes, Patrick was truly amazed, not to mention mightily relieved.

'Aw, it was too easy,' gloated Charlie as he shook the paw that was still smarting.

'Wow! Charlie, that was brilliantly done!' gushed Patrick as they were now alerted by a clawing sound coming from a metal bucket to their left.

They stared at the bucket and were amazed when they saw Sniffer climb out, jump to the floor and then shake off the excess water.

'Sniffer?—*what were you doing in there?*' asked Patrick incredulously.

'Oh never mind that, snff—we've got to get to that room up there!' Sniffer informed them, as he pointed to a door on the mezzanine floor on the other side of the warehouse. 'That's where they're keeping our friends!'

'Nice work Sniffer!' nodded Charlie; '*what are we waiting for?*'

— CHAPTER TEN —

THE ESCAPE

Sniffer guided Charlie and Patrick towards a staircase, moving quickly, fully aware that he was still being pursued by his adversaries from the sewer. They scrambled up the stairs and ran to the door that Sniffer had been pointing to. A frosted glass window at the top had the word *LABORATORY* inscribed in it. What soon became apparent was that the door was tightly shut. They were wondering how to get in when Patrick noticed an air vent, the front of which appeared to be loose. The vent was quite close to the ground and easily within reach. They climbed through and, upon doing so, the trio found themselves in a large room.

They saw tables with instruments and apparatus on them and wondered what macabre experiments had been carried out in this gruesome place. Then they looked up at the far wall close to the window and saw about ten cages sitting on top of a row of cupboards and about three feet off the ground. They were trying to make out if anyone was in the cages when a babble of excited squeaking burst forth from them.

'Over here boys,' Maisie called out.

Sniffer, Charlie and Patrick soon realised that they had found their kidnapped friends but upon looking up, Patrick also noticed B1, B2, and Ted in a cage.

'What are you three doing up there?' he asked.

'We were caught by rats,' came the disgruntled reply.

Sniffer then noticed Cedric in another cage and asked him the same question.

'I'll tell you later,' Cedric answered before adding, 'anyway, where did you get to?'

'Oh, um, snff, I'll tell you later as well—first we've got to get you all out of here!'

None of them heard the sound of the air vent opening once again but they were all startled by a voice that was immediately recognisable to Sniffer.

'This is nice—you've brought yourselves here and saved us the bother!' snarled a rat in a self-satisfied tone.

It was one of the creatures that had been chasing Sniffer, who now felt like a cornered rat himself. Charlie had other ideas though. Still *cock-a-hoop* after having *floored* the two rats downstairs, he was in no mood to take any nonsense from this scrawny rodent. With the confidence of a seasoned prize-fighter Charlie strode over and, with one swing of his right paw, he knocked the rat clean out.

A huge cheer went up from the cages but there now seemed to be a big commotion coming from outside on the balcony. Two more rats had been about to climb in through the vent when Badger and Gnasher had spotted them. The brothers had seen Sniffer, Charlie and Patrick from the other side of the warehouse and hastily headed in their direction. Upon seeing the rats they charged towards them at full speed, taking them by surprise. By the time Charlie had poked his head out to see what was going on, Badger and Gnasher were already in the process of dragging the beleaguered creatures towards the vent.

'That's three of them now!' whooped Patrick.

'If we can get everyone out we can put the rats in one of these cages,' suggested Charlie.

They were wondering how they could open the cages when Cedric pointed to a stick that the rats had used for that very purpose. The five of them pushed a chair into position below the first cage and Sniffer, stick in mouth, jumped on to it, using Gnasher as a *stepping stone*. He reached up and unlocked the cage and Cedric, followed by Bruno and Eric, strode out, grateful that his confinement was short-lived. They leapt gingerly onto the chair and then, with a helping hand from the others, climbed carefully down to the floor. The chair was pushed along to the next cage with Sniffer still on it and the process was repeated until all nineteen captives had been released. Between them they managed to lift the rats into a cage and lock them up.

Before leaving, Badger took a head count.

'There are twenty-four of us here which means we're missing three,' he concluded, noting the addition of Bruno and Eric to their number.

They quickly deduced that Bobby, Freddy and Dorie were the ones that were missing and decided to search for them as they went.

Oi, let us out of here!' came a cry from a cage above their heads.

'Enjoy your experiments!' Emily taunted them.

One by one they clambered out through the vent and assembled on the balcony.

'I think we should split into three groups and go in different directions to look for the others,' suggested Badger.

'Do you really think we should split up?' grumbled Smokey, reluctant to separate from everyone so soon after being reunited.

'Oh yes!' insisted Patrick, 'it's the way they do it in the movies!'

So it was that Pauline and daughters along with Cedric, Eric and Bruno, headed off stage right. Charlie, Patrick, Sniffer, Smokey, Sandy, B1, B2 and Ted went down the stairs and through the warehouse. Following them down the stairs before making a left turn towards the east side of the building were Badger, Gnasher, Dylan, Cyril, Boo, Emily, Joey, Lucky and Flossy.

Charlie's group soon reached the point where Sniffer had rendered the two rats unconscious thirty minutes before. He must have clattered into them heavily as they were only just starting to come round. Charlie restrained them as he implored the others to fetch an empty wooden crate from nearby.

The rats were starting to struggle. 'Much as I don't like violence...!' Charlie uttered as he slickly banged their heads together, sending them back into dreamland.

They managed to push the crate onto its side and then upend it over the comatose rats who were now imprisoned inside. They then headed for the exit close to the front door of the building but stopped in their tracks upon hearing footsteps.

'What's that noise?' asked Sandy.

'I think the sleeping man has woken up,' replied Patrick.

The footsteps were getting closer and they decided it would be prudent to hide behind boxes or anything else they could find. The man stepped into the warehouse and immediately noticed the upturned crate and the incarcerated rats.

'Funny,' he muttered to himself as he strode away towards the laboratory.

'What do we do now?' wondered Sandy.

'Get the heck out of here before we get caught,' yelled Charlie.

With no dissenting voices, they all followed Charlie and Patrick as they led them through a door into a small cupboard. It was very dark but Patrick managed to find the broken floorboard where he and Charlie had climbed in. They squeezed through, dropping down a few inches onto cold and dusty concrete. A short distance away was a small oblong of light. They soon crawled through and onto the path that ran outside along the perimeter of the building.

As the security guard was heading towards the laboratory, Pauline's group had proceeded along the balcony on the mezzanine floor and into a corridor. This led to another set of stairs that took them down and past some offices situated at the west side of the building. They were guided by the dusky light that filtered in through a row of windows close to ceiling level.

They stopped short on hearing some scampering coming from nearby. As they stood silently they could just make out the silhouettes of three rats. The shadows moved purposely forward and a voice began to speak.

'Where do you think you're going?'

'Get out of our way you little scumbags!'

The second voice was immediately recognised by the girls.

'Come on then, do you really think you can protect your two little friends?' challenged a rat.

It was obvious that they were talking to Bobby, who was bravely trying to defend Freddy and Dorie. Then they heard Freddy's voice.

'I'll help you sort them out Bobby!'

'We've got to do something,' said Eric.

Bruno suggested that they overpower the rats but Pauline thought she had a better idea and whispered something to Monica, Maisie and Tufty. With a little assistance, Pauline managed to climb onto a small table in a corner of the corridor, while Cedric, Eric and Bruno hid close by, reminding the girls that they were there if they needed them.

Then Monica boldly called out to the rats.

'Hey boys—come and get us!'

The rodent trio looked round in surprise but upon seeing Monica, Maisie and Tufty, their attention was immediately diverted. They bounded towards the girls but couldn't understand why they made no effort to run away.

'So, you're giving yourselves up are you?' one asked.

'Well, the thing is…,' gushed Maisie.

'The thing is what?' asked a rat impatiently.

'The thing is,' Monica cut in, 'you guys are kinda cute.'

'We are?' they stammered, disarmed and bemused by the unexpected compliment.

'Yes, and it would be such a shame to go back into those cages without a bit of—*kissy, kissy,*' pouted Tufty.

'So what are you waiting for boys?' Maisie asked.

'Come on then girls, we're ready,' grunted the rats.

'How about you come over here you gorgeous hunks?' purred Monica, her face belying the fact that the very thought made her feel sick.

As the rats came over, Maisie suggested that they should stand back to back, as she guided them to a spot close to the table. They were stupid enough to comply but were getting a little impatient.

'Come on then girls, let's do it,' drooled one.

'Ok,' the girls choked as they lined up in front of each rat, 'but just one thing,' insisted Monica.

'Whassat?' asked a rat.

'You've got to close your eyes.'

As the rats gullibly acquiesced, the girls tiptoed quickly but silently away. The trio of rodents were wondering what was going on and were just about to open their eyes when Pauline leapt from the table and landed squarely on all three heads. Two of them immediately fell to the ground unconscious while the third swaggered around dazed.

Pauline was just about to barge him with her rear end when he uttered, *'that was amazing!'* before falling to the floor in a crumpled heap.

'Nice work girls,' the lads called out in appreciation.

'Yes, well done,' beamed Bobby as he approached with Freddy and Dorie.

The three were quickly brought up-to-date and then it was decided that they should go back up the stairs to the balcony and out through the warehouse. This way it might be easier to find the others. They had just reached the balcony when the security guard burst out of the laboratory and was ranting to himself.

'I don't know what's going on here but I do know that Mr Fanshaw's going to go berserk!'

As he strode briskly in the direction of the guinea pigs they turned round and scrambled back the way they had just come. They ran beyond the unconscious rodents and passed out of view as they heard the man say, 'more useless rats—I might as well put them in the cages with the others.'

There was a quick change of plan and they all now followed Bobby to the east side of the building where he, Freddy and Dorie had entered a little while before. Meanwhile the security guard had returned to his desk and was on the phone to Cuthbert Fanshaw. Fanshaw's voice bellowed down the phone.

'What?—how did this happen?—were you asleep man?—right, I'm coming straight over!'

Bobby led the group down to ground level and into a small room. The room had a table and chairs and a worktop with a washbasin situated at one end. To the side of it there was a kettle and some tins and jars. Beneath was a pipe that was gaping open. When Bobby, Freddy and Dorie had climbed in through the pipe originally, their combined weight had managed to dislodge a section that linked with the washbasin waste and it now provided a handy escape tunnel. They were all soon outside and were carefully crawling towards the front of the building. Beyond the main entrance they thought they could see their friends and were about to run across when they were startled by the approach of car headlights.

Cuthbert Fanshaw only lived a five-minute drive from the factory and was just arriving. The headlights flashed across the faces of the guinea pigs. This is just like *The Great Escape* thought Charlie as they all dived for whatever cover they could find. Cuthbert Fanshaw got out of his car and ran quickly up the front steps, failing to see the guinea pigs hiding close by, as good fortune would have it.

They still didn't dare to move until Fanshaw was out of sight and as they watched him go in they heard a terrifying sound as he screeched at the security guard

'How could you let this happen?—how can someone just stroll in here and make off with fifteen guinea pigs under your very nose?'

The man tried to answer but before he could get any words out Cuthbert continued; 'have all of the creatures gone?'

'There are just six rats in the cages now,' the guard replied falteringly.

'Darn useless rats—I'm going to make them pay for this—they're going to be lab rats from now on!' Cuthbert screamed before turning to the security guard. 'By the way—*you're fired!'*

Cuthbert Fanshaw stormed into the warehouse and the guinea pigs saw this as their chance to get away. They scrambled across the front of the forecourt and round to the south side of the building so that they would be out of sight if Fanshaw came back out.

'It's a relief to see all of ya's,' sighed Patrick.

'There are only eighteen of us though,' announced Smokey.

'Badger and...,' Bobby had begun to say when Gnasher called out, 'we're over here!' Badger, Gnasher, Dylan, Cyril, Boo, Emily, Joey, Lucky and Flossy walked over to them.

'Snff, I think that's all of us now,' Sniffer calculated.

They quickly established that all twenty-seven of them were present and there now seemed little point in wasting any time. They set off in the direction of the nearest section of perimeter fence, Cedric taking up the rear as usual. They soon scrambled beneath it and there was a tangible sense of relief that they had managed to escape the confines of Fanshaw Cosmetics. There was now an eagerness to get home—so much so that none of them noticed that Cedric was no longer in their midst as they crossed the main road and headed for the cover of the grass and bushes on the other side.

They continued until they were deep enough into the bushes to feel safe before stopping to take stock of the situation.

'Oi'm not wishing to tempt fate but oi t'ink we can safely say the hard work's done—it should be *plain sailin'* from now on,' cooed Patrick.

'Don't speak too soon!' responded B1, echoing the disquiet felt by a few of the others.

CHAPTER ELEVEN

A NIGHT IN THE BARN

A single downstairs light glowed from a nearby building. The farmhouse was the one that they had passed on their way to Fanshaw Cosmetics and it now provided a helpful marker to guide them on their way. They knew that if they kept to the left and headed towards the trees in the distance, they would be on course for Whitebridge. Soon they were ready to get going.

'How long will it take us to get home?' Boo asked, dreading the thought of too much walking.

B1 answered her mother. 'It took us a day to get here, so we should be on course to arrive early morning if we set off now.'

This was going to be the ideal time as Whitebridge would not be too busy when they got there, hopefully making it far less hazardous to cross than the first time around. They began to make their way from the cover of the bushes onto a well-kept area of lawn before crossing a narrow gravel road. The road was, in fact, a long driveway that led to Postelthwaite Farm and the lawn on either side was interspersed by a row of evenly spaced tall oak trees.

It was not long before they reached a hedgerow that bordered the first field adjacent to the farm. They were about to start crawling underneath the hedgerow when they heard the sound of a dog barking from inside the farmhouse.

The door opened and Farmer Postelthwaite shouted, *'what is it Sasha—what's out there?'*

The German shepherd ran out of the house, immediately picking up the cavy scent. She was now barking even louder and the sight of such a large dog bounding towards them filled the guinea pigs with terror. They crawled under the hedge as quickly as they could. Pauline was the last of them and hadn't quite made it through when Sasha pounced. She felt sharp teeth bite into her hind paw but somehow managed to scramble clear. Sasha was still barking fiercely as she tried to poke her nose beneath the hedgerow while, on the other side, Pauline crawled gingerly away. The remainder of Sasha's quarry had scrambled a little distance into the field. Farmer Postelthwaite had now caught up with Sasha and was trying to decipher exactly what she was barking at. He could see nothing and merely assumed that she'd picked up the scent of rabbits.

'Come away now Sasha!' he commanded as he began to walk back towards the farmhouse.

Sasha continued barking for a few seconds but upon receiving a second command, reluctantly turned away, obediently following her master although looking back at the hedgerow all the while. Soon she was back indoors and the guinea pigs breathed a collective sigh of relief.

'Hopefully we'll make quick progress now,' sighed Patrick, 'come on Pauline, don't lag behind!' he urged.

He had spotted her sitting close to the hedgerow as he was speaking.

'Come on mum, what's the matter?' Tufty called out.

'You'll have to go without me—I've hurt my paw,' Pauline shouted to them.

They were all alarmed by this development. They couldn't continue and leave Pauline behind but this was a huge setback just when they thought that the coast was finally clear for them to head home. They saw that her paw was badly cut and bleeding. She had tried to walk but it was very painful for her to do so.

'What do we do now?' asked Sandy.

'We can't go home but I wouldn't fancy hanging about here all night either,' groaned B1.

It quickly became clear that they needed to find shelter as close by as possible so that they could rest for the night in the hope that Pauline's paw would be in better shape by the morning. Bobby remembered seeing a barn on the other side of the farmhouse. It should only have been a two minute walk away but it took them ten as they flanked Pauline, who crawled slowly as she dragged her paw behind her.

Once inside, they peered at the dimly lit surroundings to seek a place to rest. There were no animals in the barn save for a few birds in the eaves. It was filled with various tools but on the right-hand side were a number of bales of hay that would provide good bedding. They could stay here until it started to get light again, or until Pauline felt fit enough to resume the journey. All of them were tired and they soon settled quietly down for the night.

***

The sewer let in very little light at the best of times but now, with darkness having descended outside, Cedric could not see a thing in his smelly dungeon. He was cold and damp and even a cigarette would not have cheered him up right now. He had hurt his paws upon landing awkwardly and now he cursed the fact that he had forgotten about the open manhole cover. He was so busy trying to catch up with everyone that he wasn't looking where he was walking. It soon became evident that no one was coming back to look for him and it dawned on Cedric that perhaps his absence had gone unnoticed.

He crawled slowly along one of the concrete banks, occasionally losing his footing and sliding into the slimy, smelly liquid that flowed along the middle.

All that walking and adventuring just to end up here, Cedric thought, but this just made him even more determined that he was going to get out and *crawl* all the way back to Crickley Meadow if necessary. However, in the total darkness he soon realised that there was going to be little chance of getting out of there tonight and, with tiredness setting in, he decided that as soon as he could find a suitable place he would rest up. Not that anywhere in this God-forsaken hole could actually be deemed suitable but somewhere at least where he could lie down without the likelihood of him sliding down into the slime.

It wasn't long before he found a part of the bank that seemed a little bit wider and this is where he intended to stay for the next few hours. He tried not to think about his predicament as he lay there cold, wet, smelly and miserable. Poor Cedric indeed!

***

After a few seemingly endless yet restful hours, the first light of dawn began to seep through the high window of the barn. Bobby roused himself and moved across to where Pauline was lying.

'How's your paw?' he asked.

'The pain's eased off a little but there's still an open wound. I don't think I could walk far.'

It was evident that they would have to bide their time in the barn and Bobby now urged everyone to move deeper into the bales of hay so that they would be hidden from view should anyone enter. Now they just waited.

They were eventually alerted by the sound of a rooster.

'We could really do to get on our way before it gets too busy around here,' reasoned Patrick, 'any chance Pauline?'

'I'm afraid not!' she replied.

Just then they heard a noise on the other side of the barn door. They sat quietly and tentatively as the sound of a latch was followed by the creaking of the door. A young boy entered the barn. He was the Postelthwaites nephew and was staying with them for the week. The guinea pigs didn't dare look up in case they were seen but they could hear the boy shuffling about. He was looking for something to play with when he spotted a candle lying on a bench. After a few seconds thought, he ran out of the barn before re-appearing a couple of minutes later, this time armed with a box of matches that he had found in the farmhouse kitchen.

He went immediately to the candle and, after a few attempts, managed to stand it on its end. He now opened the box and took out a match. He struck the phosphorus tip against the side of the box and a flame appeared but as he attempted to light the candle, it fell over and dropped to the floor. He quickly blew out the flame, picked the candle up and stood it on its end again before striking another match. This time he succeeded in lighting the candle.

He stood and watched in fascination as the flame flickered. Freddy was also fascinated and had climbed up to get a closer look. Some of his companions were telling Freddy to come back when he stumbled forwards down the bale of hay and fell to the floor.

The boy turned round quickly. 'Wh...what was that!' he stuttered in surprise.

As he watched Freddy scramble back up the bale, the candle fell to the floor once again. This time it had landed among some loose strands of hay, quickly setting them alight. The boy attempted to stifle the flames by stamping on them but unfortunately they were spreading very quickly and a bale of hay was now fully ablaze. The youngster panicked when he realised that the fire was out of control and he ran to the farmhouse to get help.

By the time Farmer Postelthwaite had put on his boots and rushed out to see what was happening, the blaze had spread across half of the barn. He ran back to the house and instructed his wife to call the fire brigade before returning to see what could be done.

The guinea pigs were obviously aware that something was desperately wrong and the smoke was quickly filling the entire barn.

'We've got to get out of here!' cried Badger, who had peered up and seen the flames getting ever closer.

'Let's go or we'll all be barbecued pork!' shouted Patrick.

The way was still clear between them and the door and they hustled towards it in a panic, trying not to breath in the smoke.

'I can't move too quickly!' cried out Pauline.

Monica, Maisie and Tufty all held back to help their mum. The rest were already escaping through the open door.

'What the...?' exclaimed Farmer Postelthwaite as he glanced down at the cavy cavalry. He was too distracted by his task of trying to deal with the flames to think any more of it. His wife Beryl was standing outside the barn.

'Come away Peter—leave the fire brigade to deal with it,' she implored.

She, of course, saw the guinea pigs as they assembled on a nearby patch of lawn, trying to splutter the smoke out of their lungs and replace it with fresh air. Once over her astonishment, she counted twenty-two of them and it quickly occurred to her that these must be the Fitchetts missing pets. Once again, she reminded her husband to be careful before rushing inside to pick up the telephone. It was Mrs Fitchett who answered.

'We'll be right over!' she stammered to Beryl excitedly.

Her mood became less euphoric when she was told about the fire and the fact that only twenty-two guinea pigs had emerged from the barn.

The twenty-two cavies weren't going anywhere. They were still recovering from the smoke and, after a quick head-count, concluded that five of their number were missing.

'Pauline, Monica, Maisie, Tufty and Cedric must still be in there,' groaned Gnasher, 'we've got to go back and find them!'

'No!' cried Bobby, 'the smoke will overwhelm us now—we'll never find them!'

'Bobby's right,' agreed Badger, 'we've just got to hope they're somehow ok.'

Cyril, however, was determined to go in and rescue his dad until it suddenly dawned on him that he hadn't actually noticed Cedric's presence since they had left the factory. The others all agreed with him and realised that Cedric must have been left behind.

Badger and Gnasher glanced at each other. *'Right!'* they cried as they both sprinted off in the direction of Fanshaw Cosmetics on a mission to find Cedric.

***

Cedric had been quite uncomfortable lying down on the cold, damp, smelly concrete but eventually he managed to relax enough to forget his surroundings and dream that he was somewhere altogether nicer. When he stopped dreaming and remembered where he was it came as a huge disappointment. However, when he looked up he noticed that he was able to see daylight coming in through the open manhole cover a little way in the distance. His eyes had adjusted to the light and he was now able to make out his surroundings, albeit dimly.

Rested, and with his paws hurting a little less, he decided to get on the move again and try to find a way out. It transpired that his resting place was only a short distance from the inlet that Sniffer had escaped through the previous night. This had to be worth a try he thought as he climbed up through the inlet and along the gradually ascending pipe.

He was in total darkness once again and was feeling rather claustrophobic as he followed the twists and turns of the narrow pipe. Cedric was wondering if he would ever see the light of day again when he was suddenly dazzled by a shaft of light in the distance. He made his way towards it as quickly as he could. He crawled along the pipe but upon reaching the end he doubted his frame would be able to squeeze through the small hole in front of him. He felt slightly despondent but when he tried he was amazed by the comparative ease with which he managed it.

He found himself standing on white porcelain a little way off the ground. He was in a small room and there were two washbasins on the other side. He was wondering how he was going to get down when he heard the door opening. Without a second thought, Cedric leapt to the floor and hid behind a pipe below the porcelain. A man had come into the room and stood for a short while a few inches from where Cedric was hiding. After the man had washed his hands and left the room, Cedric noticed that the door was closing very slowly and he made a dash for it, squeezing through seconds before it slammed shut.

He was now in the warehouse and was somewhat taken aback by all the people who were busily milling round. There was no way, he firmly decided, that he was going to get caught again. He found a hiding place beneath the loading platform and made up his mind he was going to stay there until all the people left. A long night was to be followed by a long day for Cedric.

***

Badger and Gnasher were still able to run fast in spite of their recent ordeal and were halfway back to the road in the space of thirty seconds. Beryl came back out of the house and this time Sasha came with her. Although excited by the sight of the assembled guinea pigs, the dog was distracted. She had seen Badger and Gnasher making their getaway along the grass bordering the driveway.

She bounded straight off towards them, quickly catching up and grabbing Badger by the scruff of the neck with her teeth, before rushing him back. Beryl took Badger off Sasha and kept a firm grip on him as the German shepherd turned tail and gave chase once again. Gnasher had almost reached the road when Sasha's teeth stopped him in his tracks. As she rushed him back, a fire engine with sirens blazing was turning into the driveway.

Sasha reached Beryl just as the fire-fighters were alighting from their vehicle. Beryl had found a box to put Badger in and she now put Gnasher in it as well, making sure it was firmly shut so that they could not run off again. She then found some more boxes and began putting the remainder of the guinea pigs in them.

The blaze was out after about ten minutes. Farmer Postelthwaite had been watching anxiously, constantly coughing up smoke from his lungs as his eyes watered. The young boy had been looking on with trepidation, fearing the consequences of the unfolding events when the charred dust finally settled.

Mr and Mrs Fitchett arrived at the farm as the last flames were being extinguished. They jumped out of their car and ran to inspect the boxes that Beryl had pointed out to them. Mrs Fitchett was overjoyed to recognise so many of her guinea pigs but she also noticed that there were two additional creatures among them. She soon deduced that five of hers were missing and quickly worked out who they were.

'Oh no!' she exclaimed, 'that means that Pauline, Monica, Maisie, Tufty and Cedric are still in the barn!'

She ran to the firemen and asked them if they had noticed any guinea pigs inside. One of them told her that they hadn't seen any but if they *were* in the barn there was no chance that they could have survived. Mrs Fitchett was now distraught.

'I've got to go in there!' she cried but a fireman blocked the way.

'It's not safe at the moment but we will look for your guinea pigs,' he promised her.

Mrs Fitchett spent a tearful few minutes, comforted by her husband, before two firemen emerged and laid four little bundles down on the grass. She cried again as the firemen stood over the limp bodies. One of them explained that they were found by the wall of the barn not far from the door.

'Are you sure there wasn't another one?' Mrs Fitchett asked.

A fireman shook his head and she gasped, 'oh no, there must be nothing left of poor Cedric!'

Mrs Fitchett was now distraught and Mr Fitchett tried vainly to give solace as the apparent horror unfolded.

'Quick!' a fireman suddenly called out, 'I think there's some signs of life—fetch the oxygen!' he instructed his colleague.

A plastic mask was placed over Pauline's face and the oxygen released. She was soon spluttering and breathing again. The operation was repeated on the other three with the same result each time.

One fireman took off his helmet and scratched his head. 'I'm truly amazed—I didn't think anything could survive with all that smoke,' he said as he muttered something about it being a miracle.

Mrs Fitchett was still crying but her emotions were now a mixture of joy and sadness. 'Poor Cedric,' she said to her husband as she picked up Pauline and gently nursed her.

'I know,' replied Mr Fitchett, 'but we've got to take care of all the others now, especially these four—they must have been through a terrible ordeal.'

The Fitchetts loaded the boxes into their car before thanking the Postelthwaites and the firemen for all they had done.

Mrs Fitchett looked at Badger and Gnasher.

'You two are still being very naughty from what I hear!' she said in a slightly admonishing tone before adding, 'I wonder who these two belong to,' pointing to Bruno and Eric.

'You now!' laughed Beryl as the Fitchetts climbed into their car and drove off.

As they reached the end of the driveway, Mr Fitchett stopped for a moment in deep thought. It had just occurred to him how close they were to Fanshaw Cosmetics *and* there was the mystery of the two extra guinea pigs.

I wonder? he thought as he turned into the road and drove Mrs Fitchett and the boxed animals the short distance home to Crickley Meadow.

CHAPTER TWELVE

BACK HOME

The Fitchetts arrived back at Fernbrook Cottage and took the guinea pigs straight to the outhouse. There was much squeaking and excitement and the ones who had been left behind were overjoyed that their errant friends had returned. The din eventually eased off and after about fifteen minutes the returning wanderers were back in their familiar hutches. Mrs Fitchett had to prepare another for Bruno and Eric.

When they had all settled back in it was Sniffer who was acting the most excitedly of them all. This was unusual for him but Mrs Fitchett knew exactly what the problem was.

'Jessie's not had her babies yet but she's doing fine Sniffer. Don't worry—you'll be the first to know when she does.'

Sniffer fell silent and seemed much more contented. It had been such a worry for him wondering, not only if she had had the babies, but if he would ever get to see them or see Jessie again.

Mrs Fitchett was not going to put them on the garden until they had all settled back in. She double-checked on Pauline and the girls and then left the outhouse, securing it with its newly fitted locks.

Now left on their own, they had a lot of questions to ask and so many tales to tell but, amid all the excitement, there was also anguish. Misty had greeted the return of their missing friends with as much anticipation as anyone else but was now sad and very disappointed with the realisation that Cedric was not amongst them. No one had mentioned his name yet, not even Cyril, Sandy or Buttons. She felt she could not even bring herself to ask about him and so she just sat and listened, waiting for a clue.

Many a hero status was bestowed as tales of the adventure unfolded but Cedric was only mentioned for the first time in relation to the Kurt Sting incident. His name did not crop up again until they told of the escape from the factory and how Cedric somehow got lost on the way to Postelthwaite Farm.

'How could you just *lose* him?' Misty stormed.

Misty had not said a word up to now and everyone was taken aback by her sudden interjection.

'Cedric got barbecued in the barn fire!' yelped Freddy, unhelpfully.

'What…? what fire?' Misty blurted out in a panic.

'We haven't got to the bit about the fire yet but don't worry, we're certain that Cedric was separated from us before then. You can rest assured he hasn't been barbecued!' said Bobby as he cast a stern glare in Freddy's direction.

'What happened to him then?' demanded Misty.

'Well, it's hard to say really, he was with us and then—he wasn't.'

Bobby's explanation petered out feebly and Misty was too upset to say anything more.

'I think my dad will be ok, he's not the type to just give up,' Cyril tried to reassure her.

Misty took scant comfort from this and none of them spoke any more for a long while.

Later that morning, Mr Fitchett went out without telling Mrs Fitchett where he was going. After parking his car, he entered through the main door of Fanshaw Cosmetics and spoke to the receptionist. There was a brief phone call before she declared that Cuthbert Fanshaw was busy and could not see him.

'*You can't go in there!*' she yelled as Mr Fitchett ignored her and walked up to Cuthbert's office, opened the door and stormed in.

'What do you think you're doing, bursting in here like this?' demanded Cuthbert.

'*I* want to know what *you* were doing with twenty-five of our guinea pigs!' Mr Fitchett fired back angrily.

'I…I have no idea what you're talking about!' Cuthbert declared firmly after a faltering start.

Mr Fitchett was in no mood for games.

'Twenty-four of them were found close to here yesterday along with two more and I can only think of one explanation as to why— *you kidnapped them so you could use them for your lousy experiments!*'

'I do not do experiments on animals and I do not do kidnapping so kindly leave now or I will be calling the police!' threatened Cuthbert, lying through his teeth.

'Don't worry, I *am* leaving and it will be *me* who's calling the police!' blasted Mr Fitchett as he stormed out of Cuthbert's office and exited the building.

Mr Fitchett felt almost certain that his hunch about Fanshaw was correct but what he saw next confirmed his suspicions. As he was about to drive out through the factory gates he noticed Bill Nilly over to his right, unloading something from the back of his van. There, in plain view inside the van, was a lawnmower—the one that had been stolen from the outhouse.

Mr Fitchett drove straight home and told Mrs Fitchett what he suspected and then called the police. The officer who had originally attended the break-in called round shortly afterwards and Mr Fitchett told him what he suspected.

'Very interesting! If they've still got the lawnmower we may be able to link Fanshaw to the break-in and that could implicate him with the kidnap as well—*if* we can find enough proof,' said the officer.

He pointed out that it wasn't illegal for Fanshaw to conduct experiments on animals but if they could pin the kidnap on him, the resulting publicity could prove very damaging to his company's image. The officer left with the intention of obtaining a warrant to search the premises of Fanshaw Cosmetics and was hoping to pay Mr Fanshaw a visit before the day was out.

***

Cedric was still hidden away under the platform that afternoon when there was a bit of a disturbance in the warehouse. Mr Fanshaw was running across the warehouse floor and up the stairs to the laboratory. The workers didn't seem to know what was going on although one of them had mentioned that they had seen a police car outside. Cuthbert Fanshaw had been served with the search warrant and the police had decided to search outside the factory first, paying particular attention to Bill Nilly's van.

Cuthbert was now trying to place himself above suspicion and decided to quickly release the rats from their cages and stick to his story that he had ended all animal experiments. Before the police came back into the factory the rats had been released and had found their way back to the sewers. The police eventually searched the warehouse, offices and laboratory but could find nothing to link Fanshaw to the kidnap although they did want to know what the cages were for. Cuthbert explained that they had been left there from when they used to do experiments and had not been removed yet. The officers doubted his story but could find nothing to disprove it.

They then questioned him about the stolen property found on his premises.

'Fools,' Fanshaw muttered under his breath when asked about the lawnmower and spade found in the van.

'What was that Mr Fanshaw?' asked an officer.

'Oh…oh, nothing—I've no idea how they got there, you'll have to ask Starbuck and Nilly about that,' replied Cuthbert.

'We already have done but they claim to know nothing about them either—even though they were found in *their* van!'

The police left, taking the lawnmower and spade with them and Fanshaw breathed a sigh of relief, although he was kicking himself for having been so careless.

***

At Fernbrook Cottage the guinea pigs had finally been allowed out onto the garden to enjoy the evening sunshine. Mrs Fitchett was very wary but didn't like to see them cooped up in their hutches all the time. She did come out and check them at regular intervals.

The young ones were playing their usual games and even B1 and B2 were joining in with them and seemed to be having a good time. Everyone had noticed a change in the twins, who no longer acted disinterested and as if they were a little *above* everybody else.

The adults were in their usual huddles but the conversation was more frantic and excitable than usual. The stories that had been told were often repeated and seemed to become more embellished with each telling. The hero status of some of the guinea pigs grew in tandem with the stories. Many of them, especially the females, would never see Badger, Gnasher, Charlie, Patrick, Bobby and Sniffer in quite the same light again.

They would have been one big happy family but for the absence of Cedric. This affected *all* of them to an extent but poor old Misty just sat in a corner of the garden by herself, looking very sad and forlorn. Cyril came over to her to try and cheer her up but she was not really in the mood to talk to anybody. Mrs Fitchett brought some food out for them and they mostly tucked in heartily. Bruno and Eric could scarcely believe their luck. They had really *landed on their feet* and were extremely happy to have been accepted into the fold. All of them were so busy eating that no one noticed the fact that Misty ate nothing at all.

***

A few miles away Cedric was enduring the longest day of his life but eventually he noticed that there were fewer people in the warehouse and within an hour, although it felt like ten, he was quite sure that there was no one left at all. He realised the time had come for him to make his move. He edged carefully out of his hiding place and surveyed the surroundings, wondering which direction he should go in to find an exit. He was still thinking when he heard some scuffling noises coming from close by. Cedric glanced round and saw an army of rats marching in his direction.

He made a dash back towards his hiding place but one of them had spotted him and yelled, *'hey you—stop!'*

By now there must have been ten rats calling to him and, realising it was useless trying to escape, Cedric just sat there ready to give himself up.

'I'm not going to run so if you're going to lock me up, let's get it over with.'

'Are you trying to get out of here?' asked a rat.

When Cedric admitted that he was the rat said to him, 'come with us, we'll show you the way.'

'But, don't you work for Fanshaw?' Cedric asked, somewhat puzzled.

'Not anymore!' the rat replied.

'We've had enough of working for that lousy double-crosser and we're getting out of here!' grumbled another.

A rat stepped forward and told Cedric, 'we've got no argument with you guys—in fact we really admire the way you handle yourselves.'

Without further ado, Cedric followed his unlikely newfound companions out of the building, listening to their conversations on the way.

'I'm going to miss that sewer—it smelt so homely,' moaned one while another answered, 'there'll be other sewers—let's just get out of this place!'

Before long they emerged into the daylight outside.

'We're heading that way,' declared a rat, pointing to the north, 'are you coming with us?'

Cedric thanked them but said that he needed to go in the opposite direction towards Whitebridge. He took a deep breath, savouring the invigorating air outside.

'What's that horrible smell?' snarled a rat.

'It's called fresh air!' another replied.

Well I don't reckon much to it—give me my sewer and that lovely smell of s…!'

The rodent was cut short. Cuthbert Fanshaw's car had just turned into the car park and the creatures were now panicking.

'Sewage,' the rat belatedly blurted out as another gave the order to *scram*. As they all scurried off towards the fields at the back, Cedric watched them for a few seconds and then realised that he ought to get going himself. He headed off through the fence, across the road and towards Postelthwaite Farm.

CHAPTER THIRTEEN

CEDRIC'S JOURNEY

All the guinea pigs were still out in the garden at Fernbrook cottage. They were in their various huddles but everything was now fairly quiet. Even Freddy, Ted, Flossy and Dorie had tired and were now just sitting together in the middle of the lawn. Away from everyone, Misty was sitting beneath a tree between the outhouse and the cottage looking very sad and forlorn.

'What's the matter with Misty?' Dorie asked the others.

Rosie, who had just walked over at that moment, thought she had the answer.

'It's what humans call *lurve!*' Rosie's body shimmied as she exaggerated the word *love*.

'What's *lurve?*' asked Flossy, mimicking the body shimmy.

Rosie attempted to explain the concept of how two guinea pigs—or even people for that matter—might have strong feelings for each other. The children nodded although they were uncertain that they understood what Rosie meant.

Dorie then asked, 'so who does Misty *lurve?*' again with the shimmy.

'Cedric!' Rosie replied, 'so be very careful what you say to her.'

'Poor Misty!' sighed Flossy.

'I've heard that Cedric might not be *coming* home!' Dorie added unhelpfully.

'And I've heard that if he does come home they might have to put him in a hole in the ground!' Freddy weighed in with even less subtlety.

'Sssh,' whispered Rosie, gesturing to the children with her paw raised to her mouth but Misty had overheard nevertheless and she now looked sadder than ever. Patrick was nearby and had noticed his mother's reaction.

'Ignore them, they're only kids,' he tried to reassure her.

'The sad thing is they're probably right,' replied Misty.

The three youngsters came over and Dorie asked, 'what happens to you when they put you in a hole in the ground?'

'You go to a place called heaven!' answered Patrick, remembering a conversation he had once overheard.

'What's heaven like?' enquired Flossy.

'I've heard it's very nice,' remarked Patrick.

'Where *is* heaven then?' asked Freddy.

'I think it's up in the sky somewhere,' replied Misty, who vaguely remembered a chat that the Fitchetts were having with the vicar, one afternoon in the garden.

The children looked very puzzled before Flossy asked, 'wouldn't it be easier to fly there in a space rocket?'

'Where on *earth* are you going to get a space rocket from?' asked Misty incredulously.

'You could make one,' suggested Dorie.

'And how, might I ask, are you going to do that?' There was now a hint of derision added to the incredulity in Misty's tone.

'Oh, it's easy,' replied Patrick matter-of-factly, 'alls ya need is an empty washing-up liquid bottle, a piece of cardboard, a pair of scissors and some sticky tape!'

Misty suddenly felt very weary and couldn't summon enough energy to be as confused as she might otherwise have been. At this point, Patrick and the children left her on her own.

Mrs Fitchett came out, having decided to get the guinea pigs in earlier than usual as she realised they would be very tired. She noticed Misty sitting by herself and went to pick her up. Just at that moment it seemed that the first autumn leaf fell from a tree and dropped close by.

'You look very sorry for yourself—I've an idea you're missing Cedric,' she said to Misty as she picked her up without any struggle. Mrs Fitchett failed to notice what appeared to be a teardrop falling from Misty's eye.

Everyone was back in the outhouse within fifteen minutes, Tufty being the last one to be caught. She did not really consider herself to be the winner as no one could be bothered to play *catch us if you can*.

Mrs Fitchett fed them all but noticed that Misty didn't touch her food. She tried to encourage her to eat but to no avail. She told Mr Fitchett about her, suggesting that she seemed to be pining for Cedric.

Mr Fitchett was not convinced about that but he did suggest bringing Misty indoors for a while in the hope that she could be coaxed into eating. Mr and Mrs Fitchett tried everything they could think of without any success. This was a great worry to Mrs Fitchett because she knew that a guinea pigs' health deteriorated quickly without nourishment.

'Cedric will be back, just you see,' she whispered into Misty's ear before taking her back out to her hutch. As the outhouse doors were locked for the night, Misty could think only of Cedric and wondered where he was right now, hoping beyond hope that he had not come to any harm and that he would be home soon.

***

Cedric stopped for a while, enjoying the taste of freedom as well as the taste of fresh grass. It was about 7.30pm when he passed between some bushes and found himself in the grounds of Postelthwaite Farm. He was anxious to evade capture, not realising that such an eventuality would prove to be his ticket home. So when the Postelthwaites and Sasha came out of the farmhouse and walked towards their Range Rover, Cedric was filled with a sense of panic.

Sasha would not get in to the Range Rover because she was distracted by a scent that she instantly recognised. She began to bark and then bounded off in the direction of Cedric. Cedric was terrified and desperate to find somewhere to hide. Sasha was running fast and he did not have long but as he turned round he noticed a hole in the ground. There was no time to stop and think, he just ran straight for it and jumped in.

'Don't you know you're trespassing?' The voice came from a creature a little bit bigger than Cedric and with long ears.

'I don't mean to, it's just that I've got to hide from a very big dog and I didn't know where else to go,' replied Cedric.

'A very big dog eh?—well, mum's the word—we'll keep quiet till it goes away,' the rabbit assured him.

Sasha soon found the rabbit hole but could not get her nose in far enough to reach Cedric. She put her head up and barked loudly and by this time Peter Postelthwaite had managed to catch up.

'It's just a rabbit's burrow Sasha, I don't know why you're making such a fuss!' remarked Peter as he attached Sasha's lead and dragged her back to the Land Rover.

Sasha continued to whine and bark as she walked reluctantly away but eventually she jumped into the vehicle and was driven off.

When they were gone, Cedric thanked his rabbit friend.

'You're very welcome—by the way, my name's Robby.'

Cedric then introduced himself and Robby asked him where he was headed.

'To Crickley Meadow.'

'Crickley Meadow eh?—if you bump into my Uncle Hopkin can you say *hello* from me?'

'Er, yes of course,' replied Cedric as he climbed out of the hole.

Once above ground, he had a quick look around and, sensing the coast was clear, set off in the direction of Whitebridge. He was finding walking easier than expected and progress across the fields was relatively swift. Two factors contributed to this newfound fleetness of foot but neither had occurred to Cedric. The walking and the unavoidable change of diet had caused him to shed a good deal of his excess weight. More importantly, he hadn't had a cigarette for two days.

Cedric made his way through the same wooded area they had passed through the previous day. He could now see houses on the north side of Whitebridge and this gave him even greater encouragement. It was just after 8.30pm when he reached a row of fences that bordered the houses at the edge of the field. One had a picket fence which he was able to crawl through. He was careful not to be seen as he walked across the back garden and when he reached the concrete patio area he noticed a bowl of water.

'Just what I need,' he muttered as he took a good drink to quench his thirst.

He was startled when a small dog started barking from the other side of the patio door and he decided it was time to make himself scarce. This he did in the nick of time before the householder looked out of the window to see what was going on.

Cedric crawled under a wooden gate at the side of the house, through the front garden and out onto the pavement. He found himself on a very familiar-looking street with houses on either side.

Two people were walking along on the other side of the road and Cedric hid under a parked car until they were out of sight. When he thought it was safe to do so, he crawled back out and onto the pavement. He surveyed the scene for a few seconds, contemplating which direction to go in.

'Now I'm sure we came from that direction on the way, or was it that direction?' he wondered to himself out loud, as he looked first one way and then the other. He was temporarily motionless and deep in thought.

'*Gottcha!*' a voice proclaimed triumphantly as a pair of hands grabbed a startled Cedric from behind.

The voice was uncomfortably familiar to Cedric and when he was turned around, he found himself confronted by a face that would be forever etched into his memory.

'Letting Kurt Sting catch you once was careless but twice is downright stupid!' laughed the vicious youth, 'and this time you haven't got your friends here to save you!'

Cedric was terrified as Kurt Sting carried him over to the very same wall where he had tied him up the previous day. Cedric had an awful feeling of *déjà vu* as the string tightened around his paws. Kurt Sting glanced down at his shoes before searching for some rocks and stones. He then stepped back and smiled gleefully as he taunted his helpless victim.

'No one's going to spoil my fun this time!' yelped Sting as he drew back his right arm.

'Don't be too sure of that young Sting!' a man's voice pronounced as the man in question grabbed Kurt Sting by the wrist.

Police Constable Wicklow declared; 'I've heard stories about you being cruel to small animals but no one's ever caught you in the act— until now that is! Kurt Sting; I am arresting you for intent to cause harm to this small creature. You do not have to say anything but it may harm your defence if you do not now mention something which you later rely on in court. Anything you do say may be given in evidence. Do you understand?'

Kurt Sting meekly indicated that he did and the constable radioed a request for a squad car. The car, blue lights flashing, soon arrived and Kurt Sting was put inside and driven off to the police station.

PC Wicklow then untied Cedric and said to him, 'right little chap, I'm going to take you to the animal shelter just down the road—hopefully they'll find out where you belong *or* find a new home for you.'

So it was that Cedric found himself spending yet another night in unfamiliar surroundings but at least this time there were some home comforts.

***

When daylight began to shine into the room early the next morning, Cedric looked around at the rabbits and cats and other smaller animals locked up in their cages. He noticed that there was another guinea pig in a cage across the room from him.

'Hello, what's your name?' asked Cedric.

'Max,' replied the Himalayan youngster with off-white shorthaired fur and a dark patch above his nose.

'My name's Cedric—what are you doing here?'

'I was owned by a young girl but it seems she got fed up with me very quickly so they brought me here. I'm not very old you know!' moaned Max, sounding rather forlorn.

'What a shame, I do hope you find a new owner soon,' said Cedric.

'Are you looking for a new owner?' Max asked.

'No, I'm looking for my old owner!' Cedric replied.

Just then they heard the sound of a key turning in the lock and the door opened. A lady came in and pressed some buttons on an alarm panel before walking into the front office. After looking through a few papers she came into the room where the animals were.

'So you're the guinea pig that was brought in last night,' she said, looking at Cedric. 'Now wait a minute—you're an American longhair and your colours match the description of the Fitchetts missing guinea pig!'

This prompted Cedric to start squeaking very enthusiastically and the lady smiled at him.

'I'd swear you understand exactly what I'm saying! Now let's see, I think I've got their number—I'll give them a call.'

It was Mrs Fitchett who answered and then ran excitedly to tell Mr Fitchett the news.

'But what about the fire?' he reminded her.

'Perhaps he was never in the barn,' Mrs Fitchett answered.

They climbed into the car and drove to the shelter. Mr Fitchett told his wife not to get her hopes up in case it wasn't Cedric but she had already convinced herself that it was. Mrs Fitchett was opening the car door before it had fully stopped in the car park of the animal shelter and ran inside. She was so overjoyed when she saw Cedric that she let out a loud cry that Mr Fitchett could hear as he was locking the car door.

The lady got Cedric out of the cage and handed him to Mrs Fitchett. As she stroked him, he purred happily and even licked her face to show how pleased he was to see her. When Mr Fitchett came in the lady explained to them what it said in her notes about Cedric being found in Whitebridge and how he was about to be assaulted by a teenager.

'How awful! Anyway we're going to take you home now,' Mrs Fitchett whispered comfortingly.

Just then she noticed Max in a cage in the corner of the room.

'Look at him, he's beautiful!'

'His name is Max and he needs a home too,' hinted the lady.

'We can't leave him here on his own,' Mrs Fitchett cajoled her husband.

'I know he's lovely and it's a shame for him but don't you think we've got quite enough guinea pigs already?' Mr Fitchett feebly replied.

'But we haven't got a Himalayan and he would be so happy with us,' Mrs Fitchett persisted, confident of getting her husband to come round to the idea.

'Oh well, I suppose one more won't make that much difference!' surrendered Mr Fitchett.

He was resigned to the idea from the start but had gone through the motions of putting up opposition. They signed some papers and then put Cedric and Max into a carrier and took them home.

'How many have we got now?' Mr Fitchett asked on the way back.

'Thirty-three plus our three visitors,' Mrs Fitchett replied.

They soon arrived back at the cottage and took Cedric and Max indoors. Mr Fitchett had gone in first and he called out, '*thirty-six* plus our three visitors!'

'What do you mean?' Mrs Fitchett quizzed him.

'We've got thirty-six guinea pigs—Jessie's had three babies while we've been out!'

Mrs Fitchett was very excited now as she took Cedric and Max to the outhouse. When the other guinea pigs realised that Cedric had returned there was an almost deafening outbreak of squeaking. Cyril, Sandy and Buttons were ecstatic. Misty lifted up her head but was not strong enough to feel the happiness and relief that she should have done. Cedric was taken straight to Misty's hutch and put in with her in the hope that it would have a positive impact. Then Max was introduced to everyone and this started another wave of squeaking. He was put in with Badger for the time being.

Mrs Fitchett then took Sniffer indoors to see Jessie and his new offspring. They were born, as all guinea pigs are, with all their fur. There was one baby who looked just like him, having almost identical markings, another that was all black, just like Jessie and, curiously, one that was all white. Sniffer stayed with them for a while before being allowed out on to the garden along with everyone else.

It was a very happy garden that day. Cyril approached Cedric who was sitting with Misty.

'Hey dad, I've got something for you!'

Cedric looked at Cyril, who appeared to be hiding something behind his back, and wondered what it could be.

'Da, da—your cigarettes dad!' declared Cyril demonstratively, as he produced a full packet that the Fitchetts had left in his hutch in the hope that Cedric would return. Suddenly a beaming smile appeared on Cedric's face as he gleefully took the cigarettes in his paw. Everyone was watching now.

'I'm really glad you've given me these,' Cedric told him.

For once in his life, Cyril would have been more than happy to see his dad smoking a cigarette and was even preparing to offer him a light.

'I've got a surprise for you too!' Cedric announced.

He then placed the cigarettes between his front paws. As everyone looked on, he crushed the pack with admirable strength before tossing it into the air and kicking it expertly into a bin that was standing a few feet away.

They all looked on in astonishment as Cedric declared, 'I don't need them anymore—I've kicked the habit!'

The astonishment quickly turned to cheers of congratulation as Cedric told everyone how he had gone without cigarettes for more than three days and had felt better for it. He also praised Bruno for giving him the inspiration to give up.

The atmosphere in the garden was one of joy but Cedric now had another worrying distraction. He was glad to be home but the relief and joy that Cedric felt was overshadowed by a problem that needed tackling very soon.

CHAPTER FOURTEEN

BETTER TIMES

The cavies played and sat in the garden but Cedric stayed with Misty and never moved from her side, except to bring her lettuce, greens and tomatoes from the selection that Mrs Fitchett had put out at dinnertime. All the while he talked to Misty, coaxed her and did everything he could to encourage her to eat.

'You are glad to see me aren't you?' Cedric asked.

'Yes of course I am, I just feel so weak,' she replied, her voice sounding frail.

'Then you must eat something!' Cedric insisted.

She protested, saying that she felt too weak to eat although Cedric pointed out that if she didn't eat she would get weaker still.

Cedric was touched by Misty's plight and the hard times he had endured in his own life, not least his recent trials, brought out a philosophical side to his character.

'There were many times on my adventure,' he began, 'when I wasn't sure if I'd ever make it home. When I got left behind I didn't know if I would ever see any of my friends again. I thought about the things I'd miss, like the garden, Mr and Mrs Fitchett, my children. Adversity really focus's your mind and, after a while, you begin to realise what matters most in your life. You know Misty, I'm so glad to be here with you now. I've come to realise now that, what I'd have missed most of all.'

'And what is that?'

'It's you Misty—*you!*'

'Do you really mean that?'

'Yes, I really do!'

'You're not just saying all this to make me feel better?' Misty asked with understandable scepticism.

'Look at me Misty—do you really think I'm making all this up?'

Misty didn't answer him but she suddenly felt a warmth that she hadn't experienced for some time and she even dared to let a little feeling of optimism creep in.

After they had been sitting there for a short while, Maisie and Tufty decided to come over and see Cedric.

'Hey, hero boy, are you coming to play with us?' asked Maisie.

Misty braced herself. *This is it!* she thought as she waited for Cedric to take them up on their offer.

'Sorry girls, I'm busy at the moment—maybe another time,' he told them as he remained firmly by Misty's side.

This came as a pleasant surprise and a great relief to Misty who really needed the support that Cedric was giving her right now. Most of all she needed to eat and Cedric began encouraging her to have some lettuce with him. He took one piece in his mouth and gently coaxed Misty into putting a piece in hers.

She really wanted to chew it but found it difficult because she hadn't eaten for so long. Cedric tried the same with greens and tomatoes but to no avail. He was desperately disappointed but just snuggled up to her. They sat together in silence for some time and the other guinea pigs left them to be alone. Misty realised that she now had everything to live for and felt that she must try and eat something, as she desperately wanted to become strong again. She was so happy to have Cedric back and didn't want to lose out on the opportunity to spend time with him now.

The Fitchetts came out into the garden to make the most of the sunshine and to watch the guinea pigs playing happily. They were very glad to have them all back but were also extremely relieved that Chloe's guinea pigs were safe and sound. How on earth would they have explained to Chloe and her family that they had managed to lose B1, B2 and Ted?

'We still don't have a name for these two,' said Mrs Fitchett pointing to Bruno and Eric although she could not have known that these were their names.

Just then the police officer dealing with the break-in came round to the back garden with another man. He introduced the man as a former security guard who had worked at Fanshaw Cosmetics and who claimed that Cuthbert Fanshaw was planning to start animal experiments again. He said that Fanshaw had acquired fifteen guinea pigs for that very purpose but they had subsequently managed to escape. He had been on duty when the escape took place and was sacked as a result of this. He now felt aggrieved and was prepared to try and identify those animals to help bring evidence against Fanshaw.

'How did they escape?' asked Mrs Fitchett.

'I'm not really certain but I'm quite sure there were no people involved in rescuing them!' replied the man.

'There, what did I tell you!' yelled Mr Fitchett who then added, 'but wait a minute—fifteen? There were twenty-five of our guinea pigs plus these two!' he exclaimed, pointing to Bruno and Eric.

The man assured him that there were definitely only fifteen at Fanshaw Cosmetics and this set Mr Fitchett's mind racing once again while the ex-security guard set about trying to identify them.

'Ah yes, Bruno and Eric, I definitely remember them because they came in last—they were unwanted by their previous owners,' the man informed them.

'So that's Bruno and that's Eric!' noted Mrs Fitchett.

Pauline and her three daughters, by now completely recovered from their ordeal, were easily identified, as were Smokey and Sandy.

'That proves that Fanshaw kidnapped our guinea pigs *and* that he was responsible for the break-in,' whooped a delighted Mr Fitchett.

Joey was soon picked out because of her distinctive eye patches but the man was having trouble with the other six. He remembered that three of them were very hairy and then picked out Cyril when he spotted his ginger coat. He was now looking for two hairy ones and three shorthaired black and white ones but it was difficult to single them out from amongst the others.

'Was he one of them?' asked Mrs Fitchett as she pointed to Cedric.

The man was quite definite that Cedric was not amongst them but he did soon pick out Dylan and Lucky. He was really struggling with the other three when suddenly Boo, Emily and Flossy moved away from the rest and stood in front of the man.

'Do you know, I'm sure it's these three, in fact, yes it definitely is,' he declared as everyone looked on in astonishment.

'It's as if they were trying to help you,' beamed Mrs Fitchett.

Having now got a positive identification, the officer explained that the case against Fanshaw was looking very strong.

As the visitors left Mr Fitchett turned to his wife and exclaimed, *'It's incredible!'*

'I know—it's wonderful to think that Fanshaw's finally going to get his comeuppance!'

'No, I don't *mean* that,' said her husband.

'Then what *do* you mean?'

'I mean that the other twelve that went missing can't have been kidnapped at all. It's my belief that they actually set off from here to rescue the ones that were captured!'

Mrs Fitchett's first thought was that this sounded impossible but Mr Fitchett challenged her to come up with an alternative explanation. It sounded incredible to him too but all the evidence seemed to lead to the same conclusion. There was the gap behind Sniffer's Rock that would allow them to escape and the sighting of guinea pigs on the road beyond Billings Farm. There was also the escape from the laboratories in which the security guard was adamant that no people were involved. What other way was there of explaining how twenty-six of them were found together at Postelthwaite Farm? Mrs Fitchett had to agree that the evidence seemed compelling and she was certainly more than happy to believe that so many of her guinea pigs could be heroes.

The Fitchetts continued to watch their pets at play in the garden and felt pleased about the way that everything had turned out. There was still the worry of Misty but they were glad that Cedric was doing his best to comfort her. Then they noticed that Cedric had taken a piece of lettuce in his mouth and, offering the other end to her, Misty took it and began to chew very tentatively. Cedric then got Misty to have some greens and tomatoes and it was encouraging and heart-warming to see.

The Fitchetts hoped that this would be the start of the road to recovery for Misty and so it proved to be. She had some more to eat a little later as well as chewing a little grass and when she came in she ate some muesli as well. Cedric was in the hutch with her now and, with him by her side, she would get stronger over the next few days.

Jessie's babies were also getting stronger each day and a little more independent. The Fitchetts had now named them all. The boy was called Monty and the black and the white girls Abbey and Peaches respectively.

Mrs Fitchett was feeling so happy about the way things had turned out that she impulsively suggested having a party when Chloe's family got back. Mr Fitchett thought that it was a great idea and was looking forward to it already. He always welcomed any opportunity to get out his harmonica and play a few tunes.

When the guinea pigs heard about the party they were very excited. Cedric further encouraged Misty.

'You'll have to keep up with your eating and get your strength up because I want you with me at this party.'

Miffy had overheard Cedric and hoped that Bobby would be similarly forthcoming but, alas for her, he was not.

Rosie still spent a lot of her time in the garden mixing with the others and joining in every conversation she could but everyone had noticed the amount of time she had been spending with Eric recently.

As soon as she heard about the party she went straight to him and declared, 'I want somebody to take me to this party—no actually, I want *you* to take me to this party El.'

'In that case I will be delighted to escort you,' he replied.

The guinea pigs had so much to look forward to now and the three days until the party seemed to take an age in passing. B1, B2 and Ted were quite happy because they were enjoying themselves so much but they knew that after the party they would be going home. Not that they weren't looking forward to seeing Chloe and sitting in their own hutches, but they would miss all their friends and the garden at Fernbrook Cottage.

'At least we're going to be indoors when the winter comes,' said B1 to B2, looking for consolation to ease the prospect of their departure.

Charlie and Patrick decided to ask Maisie and Tufty respectively to come to the party with them and even had a bet with the other as to which one would succeed.

'For cavy honour!' they chanted as they clapped their raised right paws together. They approached the girls, feeling less confident than they looked and Charlie was first up.

'Go to the party with you?—of course I will,' Maisie answered.

Charlie was surprised and delighted by the response and looked to Patrick to claim the honour of winning the bet. He was surprised once again when he heard Tufty say, 'I'd *love* to go to the party with you Patrick—I thought you'd never ask!'

On the Sunday morning, Mr Fitchett got a phone call from the police informing him that Cuthbert Fanshaw was being sent for trial in October for being a party to burglary and the theft of thirteen guinea pigs. Bill Nilly and Brian Starbuck were being charged with carrying out the offences. Mr Fitchett was also informed that his lawnmower and spade would be returned to him after the trial. The Fitchetts were pleased with the news about Cuthbert Fanshaw, as they knew it meant that he would be unlikely ever to carry out experiments on animals again and, if Fanshaw Cosmetics went out of business, Fanshaw would have no one to blame but himself.

Mr Fitchett was sitting at the kitchen table drinking a cup of tea when he glanced at the previous evening's *Whitebridge Gazette*. The name *Kurt Sting* leapt out from the page. Neither he nor Mrs Fitchett had noticed the story the night before but he was now reading about how Sting was being sent to trial on a charge of animal cruelty. Mr Fitchett read on intently and with heightened interest when he realised that the animal in question was a guinea pig.

Cedric! he thought to himself after checking that the date correlated. Sting had admitted to a similar attempted assault on the same animal the previous day but claimed that a group of guinea pigs had come to the aid of the stricken creature on that occasion.

'This is fantastic!' announced Mr Fitchett after reading the story to his wife. 'This has to be proof that our guinea pigs were in Whitebridge on the day of the break-in!'

'Then they *must* have gone to rescue the others!' gushed an incredulous but very proud Mrs Fitchett.

CHAPTER FIFTEEN

THE PARROT

The party was set for the August Bank Holiday Monday, a week to the day since the arrival at Fernbrook Cottage of B1, B2 and Ted. Preparations were well under way although it wasn't going to be a big affair. Chloe and her family would be there of course, as well as Mr and Mrs Naylor who lived next door. The vicar had been invited along with Mrs Cosgrove who helped out at the church. Mrs Fitchett's brother, Tom Beaumont and his wife, Louise were coming from Lambourne while Mr Fitchett's friend Gerald from Over Stanley was invited too. There was also the small matter of thirty-nine guinea pigs that were going to be enjoying the party atmosphere, not to mention the extra rations of vegetables that would be on offer.

Mrs Fitchett made sure that she had enough food in for the buffet and enough tea and coffee to go round. Mr Fitchett bought a bottle of sherry and a bottle each of red and white wine.

'You had better go easy on that stuff!' warned Mrs Fitchett, remembering how her husband had got a little carried away the previous New Year's Eve.

'Of course I will,' Mr Fitchett assured her, insisting that it was for the benefit of the guests.

The day of the party soon arrived and the Fitchetts got up early to prepare everything. The buffet included sandwiches with various fillings as well as a selection of cheeses and other savoury items. There were also salads and dips and biscuits and cakes and chocolate gateaux to finish off with.

It was a beautiful sunny day again. Mr Fitchett set up the stereo on the patio and as soon all the preparations had been completed, the guinea pigs were let out onto the garden.

'This is going to be a great party!' chirped Freddy.

'Do you think we'll get extra portions of lettuce and things?' Dorie asked.

'Oo-er, what's that thing over there?' wondered Emily, pointing to the stereo.

'That's to play music on so that we can dance to it,' replied Mandy.

'I'm so looking forward to this!' exclaimed Rosie excitedly, 'we're going to have a dance aren't we El?'

'Oh—er, yes, I suppose so,' answered Eric tentatively.

They played their usual games and did their usual things but, with the party due to start in an hour, there was a tangible air of excitement.

Chloe's family were the first to arrive and the young girl rushed straight out into the garden to find B1, B2 and Ted. She was very glad to see them and they likewise, to see her. Neither Chloe or her mum and dad knew anything of the events of the past week. The Fitchetts hadn't dared to contact them when they first went missing and didn't want to worry Chloe while she was on holiday.

They had decided to save the story of the kidnap and the rescue mission as it would certainly make a great party-piece, but first they would wait until all the guests had arrived. They did not have to wait very long. First Mr and Mrs Naylor popped over from next door followed in quick succession by Tom and Louise, and Gerald. When the vicar arrived soon afterwards, bringing Mrs Cosgrove with him, the party was ready to begin.

Very soon there was music playing and the guests were chatting on the patio and drinking either tea or coffee.

'Look at all those hamsters running round your garden Richard!—don't they drive you mad?' Tom asked his brother-in-law.

'They're guinea pigs actually!' Mr Fitchett corrected him.

'But they must take up so much time and I bet they cost a fortune as well. Why don't you just give them away?' added Tom.

'They make great pets and I can assure you that these guinea pigs are very special,' Mr Fitchett replied, although Tom remained unimpressed.

'Hey, Phyllis!' Tom called out to his sister, 'you've certainly got your husband brainwashed with these hamsters of yours!'

'They're *guinea pigs*—now behave yourself Tom!' Louise admonished him.

'Hamsters, guinea pigs, it's all the same to me. Pity you don't have a barbecue Richard, I'm sure they'd taste a treat, ha, ha!' laughed Tom, who was beginning to get on the nerves of some of the guests.

'You've got to remember Tom, they are all God's creatures!' observed the vicar who then added, 'mind you, I do believe they are something of a delicacy in certain parts of the world!'

'Now, now vicar, you're being a bit naughty—they seem like delightful little creatures to me,' said Mrs Cosgrove.

'They are delightful *and* very intelligent!' spluttered Chloe indignantly.

She was backed up by her mum and dad and the Fitchetts.

'In fact, we've got a few tales to tell you about our guinea pigs,' Mr Fitchett informed the partygoers.

'Tails?' quipped Tom, 'but I thought they didn't have tails! ha, ha, ha!'

Mrs Fitchett began by telling everybody about the break-in and about how twenty-four guinea pigs went missing.

'You mean B1, B2 and Ted went missing as well?' interrupted Chloe as she and her parents were taken aback.

The Fitchetts were somewhat embarrassed by the admission but assured the family that the three were absolutely fine now. The two hosts took it in turns to tell the story of the kidnap and rescue as the guests all listened intently. When they finally finished there was a short silence before Tom reacted with predictable cynicism.

'You two certainly know how to tell a story—very entertaining!'

'It's all absolutely true Tom!' Mr Fitchett assured him.

'Oh come on! You don't honestly expect us to believe these fairy stories do you?' Tom replied.

'But what we've told you are the facts,' Mrs Fitchett insisted.

'I don't know which of you two is more bonkers!' said Tom.

The vicar was more diplomatic.

'It *is* all very fascinating and I'm convinced you're telling the truth as you see it but surely there must be another explanation.'

Mr Fitchett appreciated that it must be difficult for anybody to accept the story but challenged him to come up with an alternative theory. The vicar became very pensive and was obviously trying very hard to put a different spin on the events. Try as he might he was unable to rise to Mr Fitchett's challenge.

'I can believe it!' declared Mrs Cosgrove, 'they seem like very intelligent creatures to me.'

The Naylors sat on the fence, secretly believing the story to be hokum but not wishing to upset their neighbours. Gerald did admit that he found the story difficult to believe but echoed Mrs Cosgrove's opinion that the guinea pigs seemed very intelligent.

'Don't tell me you believe any of this rubbish Louise!' Tom asked his wife.

'As a matter of fact I do! I'm sure Richard and Phyllis are telling us the truth and the facts seem to bear out their explanation!' she replied.

'Crikey!' groaned Tom, 'I think I might regret coming to this party—my wife's gone barmy as well now!'

Chloe's family believed the story and were very proud of all the guinea pigs.

The guests were now talking among themselves but the Fitchetts story was the only topic of conversation. Tom asked Mr Fitchett to show him where the guinea pigs escaped from. He took Tom down to Sniffer's Rock and lifted it up to reveal the gap in the fence behind. He explained to Tom that he believed the rock must have been dislodged when the intruders climbed over the fence. Tom spotted a piece of wood and a brick that were lying close by.

'I'm just amazed you haven't suggested that the hamsters used that bit of wood and brick to lever the rock away!' laughed Tom in sarcastic jest.

The thought had never occurred to Mr Fitchett but this now set his mind racing again. However, he did not wish to invite any more jibes and said nothing to Tom.

While Tom and Mr Fitchett were having their conversation, Chloe had asked Mrs Fitchett if she could bring Jessie and her babies outside for a while. She was told that the babies could come out until everybody went inside for the buffet but Jessie could stay out a bit longer. It was the first time that Monty, Abbey and Peaches had been introduced to the other guinea pigs and it was a very proud moment for Sniffer. Everyone enquired after Jessie's health and she told them she was doing fine and hoped to be back in the outhouse soon.

'They're such beautiful babies!' purred Misty.

'Hey, nice work Sniffer!' enthused Cedric, patting him heavily on the back, 'you'll be catching up to me at this rate!'

'Oh, I don't know about that!' Sniffer replied with sheepish embarrassment.

Tom and Mr Fitchett were walking back across the garden to the patio when Tom asked why the *hamsters* were all gathered together.

'They've come to see the new babies,' Mr Fitchett answered.

'This hamster thing is really getting to you isn't it Richard?' Tom replied.

Just then Mr Fitchett noticed that Gerald was getting his banjo out of its case and so he decided to go back into the cottage to find his harmonica. First though, he offered his guests something a little stronger in the way of a beverage. Tom, as well as the vicar, Gerald and Chloe's dad opted for red wine while the Naylors, Chloe's mum and Mr Fitchett himself had a glass of sherry. Mrs Cosgrove and Mrs Fitchett continued to drink tea. No one noticed Mr Fitchett downing his first glass of sherry quickly for a little *Dutch courage* ahead of his performance, before pouring himself a second one. He put the glass of sherry down on the patio and he and Gerald launched themselves into playing a few tunes. After a tentative start they began to enjoy themselves immensely.

'They're very good aren't they,' commented Mrs Cosgrove.

'The music's nearly as good as the stories!' mocked Tom.

The duo planned to perform one more piece before everyone went indoors for the buffet. They were now playing very enthusiastically and Mr Fitchett was dancing as he played. He was doing a sideways jig when he accidentally knocked his sherry over, spilling the contents onto the patio though luckily not breaking the glass.

'Right, that's it Richard Fitchett!'

Mrs Fitchett decided it was time to curb her husband's bohemian streak and invited the guests indoors for the buffet. As they filed in, Chloe went to fetch the babies to bring them in and Mr Fitchett pressed the play button on the stereo.

Now it was the guinea pigs turn to party!

'Shall we take the first dance El?' Rosie asked. It was more of a command than a question

'Oh, er, yes, I suppose so,' Eric replied, not really having any say in the matter.

The *dance floor*, an area of patio between the fishpond and the lawn, filled up quickly. Tufty was happy to dance with Patrick while

Maisie managed to drag Charlie on. Soon a few of the girls and most of the children were up dancing. There was Pauline, Emily, Mandy, Gracie, Buttons, Lucky and Smokey, the latter not dancing too vigorously in case her tuft became dishevelled.

It was not long before Cyril surprised everyone by taking to the dance floor and enjoying himself immensely. No one could remember him being so relaxed and Boo took the opportunity to join him, staying with him the whole time they were dancing. Pauline was having a really good time, enjoying herself so much that she was shaking her rear with potentially dangerous gusto.

Misty, now in far better health, was having a great time although she didn't want to dance. She was content to sit and watch with Cedric. Even Badger and Gnasher eventually took to the dance floor although not with anyone in particular and, it must be said, none too gracefully.

There were quite a mixture of songs on the stereo, some fast and some slow but all of them danceable. Next up was *Bobby's girl*, a favourite of Mrs Fitchett. Miffy picked up on the words of the song immediately and sunk into a daydream as she listened. As the refrain rang out she imagined that Bobby had come up to her and was asking her to dance. As she listened to the words, *I wanna be...Bobby's girl*, she was in a trance and imagined that she could hear Bobby saying, *could I have the pleasure of this dance Miffy*. Again she heard the words before she suddenly snapped out of her daydream.

'Could I have the pleasure of this dance Miffy?' Bobby asked, as he stood right there in front of her.

'Oh..., yes of course you can Bobby!' Miffy replied, hardly able to believe her eyes and ears.

'For a while there I thought you were ignoring me,' joked Bobby as they took to the dance floor.

Sniffer had been very reluctant to dance but was eventually persuaded by Jessie to smooch to a slower song. A faster song followed and he declined to continue, leaving Jessie to dance with the other girls. He ambled across the patio so that he could walk around the dancers but stopped when he noticed some liquid. It was, in fact, Mr Fitchett's spilled sherry. Sniffer didn't know what it was but decided he liked the smell and proceeded to lick it all up.

When he had finished he suddenly felt the urge to carry on dancing after all. The next song was also a fast one and from the first beat Sniffer launched himself into a furious frenzy. He was soon in amongst the other dancers and they were amazed to see how much energy he displayed. They also found him very amusing—except when he bumped into them!

'I don't know what's got into Sniffer!' said Mandy.

'Perhaps he's celebrating his new litter,' suggested Gracie.

Sniffer continued dancing for song after song and Jessie warned him to be careful as he continued to bump into the other dancers. However, when he bumped into Pauline it was she who got the better of the encounter, her rear end launching him across the patio. As he ended up close to the fishpond, Jessie looked on with great concern. She was relieved to see him get up again and he continued to dance right on the spot where he had landed.

All the guinea pigs were up dancing now to the next song. Even Misty and Cedric got up for this one and, as Barry White's words rang out, *can't get enough of your lurve babe,* they all shimmied together. All the while Sniffer was edging closer and closer to the fishpond without realising it. No one noticed until Jessie looked up and shouted a vain warning. It came too late! Sniffer had tumbled backwards and fallen in.

'Oh no!' cried Jessie, *'Sniffer's going to drown—somebody save him!'*

They all stopped dancing and assembled around the pond. No one could see Sniffer but Gnasher had dived straight in. He soon found his dad and pushed him upwards to the pond's edge. As Sniffer's nose became visible above the surface of the water, Badger reached in and grabbed his paw, pulling him out as the others looked anxiously on. Badger then gave a helping paw to Gnasher who was also soon on dry land. The two wet guinea pigs shook of the excess water—something that was getting to be a habit for Sniffer—and everyone breathed a collective sigh of relief.

The party guests were now reappearing and Tom wondered what all the hamsters were doing on the patio.

'Perhaps they've been dancing,' suggested Mrs Naylor, tongue in cheek.

'That'll be it!—silly me for not thinking of that!' announced Tom in mock self-chastisement.

Mr Fitchett turned the stereo off and Chloe went to collect B1, B2 and Ted. The three had really enjoyed themselves and had had an incredibly exciting stay but they realised that the time had now come for them to go. They felt very sad to be leaving all their friends but were also looking forward to going home to their own hutches.

The guests were all leaving now and, when the vicar had said his goodbyes and thanked Mr and Mrs Fitchett, he turned to the guinea pigs and called goodbye to them in partial jest. He was a little surprised when they responded by squeaking very loudly as he and Mrs Cosgrove left. Next to exit were the Naylors and Gerald who likewise, offered their farewell to the guinea pigs and received the same response.

'It's as if they're saying goodbye to us,' laughed Mrs Naylor.

When Chloe's family departed the squeaking was louder than ever.

'You've nearly got me believing they're actually saying goodbye!' japed Tom as he himself shouted a speculative farewell to the assembled creatures.

He waited for a response but there was none, just complete silence. Even the unflappable Tom didn't quite know what to make of it. For once in his life he felt slightly uncomfortable when, out of the silence came an unusual sound. The cocktail of wine and pond water had unsettled Sniffer's stomach a little and he suddenly let out a loud burp. Upon hearing it all of the guinea pigs burst into hearty laughter.

'See, they do love me after all!' declared Tom as he and Louise left Fernbrook Cottage to signal the end of the party and the end of a very eventful week.

CAVY FAMILY TREE

***

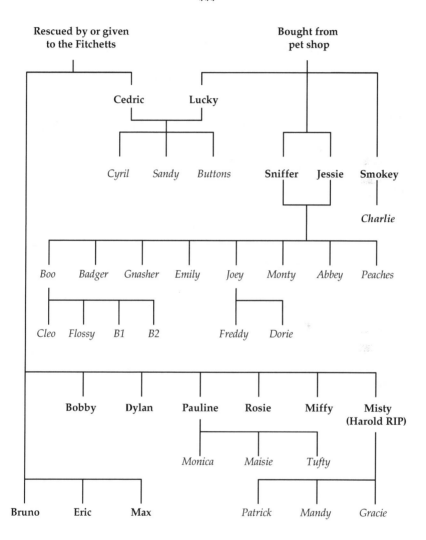

Rescued by or given to the Fitchetts

Bought from pet shop

Cedric — **Lucky**

Cyril *Sandy* *Buttons*   **Sniffer** — **Jessie**   **Smokey**

Charlie

Boo *Badger* *Gnasher* *Emily* *Joey* *Monty* *Abbey* *Peaches*

Cleo *Flossy* *B1* *B2*   *Freddy* *Dorie*

Bobby **Dylan** **Pauline** **Rosie** **Miffy** **Misty (Harold RIP)**

Monica *Maisie* *Tufty*

Bruno **Eric** **Max**   *Patrick* *Mandy* *Gracie*

Cavies named in *italics* were born at Fernbrook Cottage